"Rebecca Li's *Illumination* is a luminous guide to a profoundly positive approach to living. One feels her trust in the natural goodness of her readers and in their ability to know it themselves. She elegantly weds the ancient teachings on Silent Illumination to contemporary life, and her own wise voice with the voices of her teachers, including the venerable Chan Master Sheng Yen."

— BEN CONNELLY, Soto Zen priest and author of *Inside Vasubandhu's Yogacara* and *Mindfulness and Intimacy*

"How can we cultivate moment-to-moment clarity to experience the peace that is always available to us, no matter what is happening? This book is like warm-hearted encouragement and support from a trusted friend who travels with us on the path of spiritual transformation."

— MUSHIM PATRICIA IKEDA, Buddhist teacher and author

"As a young meditation student, Rebecca Li was told by her teacher, Master Sheng Yen, that she would help a lot of people. She is certainly doing that. In this timely and beautiful book—coming at a moment of deep complexity in our world—Rebecca offers us an essential practice and an important reminder: meditation at its core, rather than being a process of striving and elimination, can be a transformative practice of bringing openhearted curiosity to the totality of our moment-to-moment experience just as it is. She reminds us that the capacity to sit with full and openhearted attention is already the fruit of the practice that we have been so desperately striving for. *Illumination* is a treasure of the heart that you will return to again and again as you walk your path. I know I certainly will."

— BROTHER PHAP HAI, Senior Dharma Teacher in the lineage of Zen Master Thich Nhat Hanh and author of *The Eight Realizations of Great Beings*

A GUIDE TO THE BUDDHIST
METHOD OF NO-METHOD

ILLUMINATION

REBECCA LI

SHAMBHALA

Shambhala Publications, Inc.
2129 13th Street
Boulder, Colorado 80302
www.shambhala.com

Cover art: Chris Zielecki / Stocksy
Cover design: Jason Alejandro
Interior design: Kate Huber-Parker

9 8 7 6 5 4 3 2 1

First Edition
Printed in the United States of America

Shambhala Publications makes every effort
to print on acid-free, recycled paper.
Shambhala Publications is distributed worldwide by
Penguin Random House, Inc., and its subsidiaries.

Library of Congress Cataloging-in-Publication Data
Names: Li, Rebecca (Professor), author.
Title: Illumination: a guide to the Buddhist method of no-method /
Rebecca Li, Ph.D.
Description: Boulder: Shambhala, 2023.
Identifiers: LCCN 2022051368 | ISBN 9781645470892 (trade paperback)
Subjects: LCSH: Enlightenment (Zen Buddhism) | Meditation—
Buddhism. | Zen Buddhism—Essence, genius, nature.
Classification: LCC BQ9288 .L53 2023 | DDC 294.3/442—dc23/
eng/20221205
LC record available at https://lccn.loc.gov/2022051368

Dedicated with deep gratitude to my teachers:
Chan masters Sheng Yen,
John Crook, and Simon Child

Silently and serenely, one forgets all words,
Clearly and vividly, it appears before you.
When one realizes it, time has no limits.
When experienced, your surroundings come to life.
Singularly illuminating is this bright awareness,
Full of wonder is pure illumination.[1]

—Master Hongzhi, "Silent Illumination"

Stay with that just as that. Stay with this just as this.[2]

—Master Hongzhi, "Practice Instructions"

CONTENTS

12

FORGETTING-EMPTINESS MODE

Resisting the True Nature of Reality

13

ALLOWING WHAT IS AND BEING FULLY HERE

ILLUMINATION

INTRODUCTION

The First Encounter

I will always remember the first retreat I attended with Master Sheng Yen, my root teacher in whose Chan lineage I received Dharma transmission and now teach as well. I traveled from Southern California to Queens, New York, to attend the seven-day meditation intensive. I had very little idea about what I was getting into, but I was happy that after my third attempt I was finally accepted. In those days, retreats were held at the Chan Meditation Center, which could accommodate only thirty people. There were just four sessions each year and most participants were regulars, which meant there were few available seats for new applicants.

Up until then I'd been meditating with a Chan group in Riverside, California, that met weekly. When I joined them for the first time, someone spoke about their experience at a retreat with Master Sheng Yen. I cannot remember what they said, but I do remember thinking, "I want to go." That thought brought me to New York a year later. The retreat schedule was rigorous. What I struggled with most was waking up at four o'clock in the morning, which was one o'clock in California. Since I was a night owl, we were rising at around the time I usually went to bed! For days, I struggled with drowsiness and jet lag. I did my best to follow the instructions on how to use the method of following the breath to meditate. I could not understand most of what Master Sheng Yen said because my Mandarin was not good enough, and he spoke with an accent that made it so difficult for me to follow that I had to rely on the translator of the Dharma talks.

Looking back at this first retreat, it is not the meditation that stands out but the two things that happened that changed the course of my life. The first was during my private interview with Master Sheng Yen. The interview room was in a small house in a courtyard behind the meditation hall. As instructed, I waited outside until the retreatant ahead of me emerged, then entered the room and made three prostrations. Then, I began to cry. The thought that came to me was "I finally found you, Shifu!" The joy and relief I experienced in that moment was like when I was a small girl and got separated from my mother in a crowded Hong Kong market and then found her again. I could not explain it, but I had the distinct feeling that I had been searching for Master Sheng Yen, waiting for just that moment, for a very long time. It was odd because I had not been looking for a Buddhist teacher. The Dharma just kind of showed up in my life, yet the intensity of that encounter remains with me many years later. There was (and is) no doubt in my mind that Master Sheng Yen was my teacher; I never felt the need to explore others.

The second life-changing event occurred at the end of that first retreat when each participant was asked to share their experience. I was sitting in the back of the room, letting others go before me. Because my Mandarin was not good, when my turn came, I spoke in English. I do not remember what I said, but what stood out was Master Sheng Yen's reply as he looked directly into my eyes: "You are going to help a lot of people." I understood I was supposed to help people as a practitioner, but I had no clue how I would go about doing so—at the time I was a graduate student studying sociology and on track to becoming a professor.

Year after year, I returned to Queens for more retreats. Although I loved (and still love) the sunny weather in Southern California, when it was time to look for an academic position, my strong affinity with Master Sheng Yen led me to accept a job in New Jersey because of its proximity to his meditation center in New York. It was during one of my many visits there that I heard about John Crook.

In my limited exposure to Chinese Buddhism up to that point, all the masters were monks. This left me with the impression that serious practice could only be done by monastics. After my first retreat, I had contemplated the possibility of entering the monastic life, but decided that the lifestyle would not suit me. Studying with a married couple in California at that time also gave me the hope that it was possible to practice seriously as a householder. When I heard that Master Sheng Yen had given Dharma transmission to a Westerner named John Crook, I was intrigued. This was a radical act— giving permission to teach to a Westerner who was not even a monastic.

As you can imagine, I was curious about John Crook long before I first met him. It was a big deal that Master Sheng Yen made him his first lay Dharma heir. In our tradition, this means he'd received a direct mind-to-mind transmission reaching like an unbroken thread all the way back to the Buddha, endorsing him to continue the Chan legacy. John Crook had been tasked by our teacher with developing a way to communicate Chan in a manner that is accessible to the Western-educated mind, and he took Master Sheng Yen's request very seriously.

Although I'd been practicing meditation for about five years and had been recruited for and considered the monastic path on several occasions, I continued not to take this route. After careful consideration I was certain I wanted to live in the world, work as a college professor, and get married—yet I still knew my calling was to share Chan teachings and the Dharma. I was happy to help Master Sheng Yen offer Chan in the West by serving as his translator. That was my favorite task as a volunteer, and it was one of my life's greatest blessings to help in that manner. Still, John Crook intrigued me: *could a layperson practice Chan well and share the Dharma in a meaningful way?* This was during the years before we would look up everything on the internet, and I was unaware of the many lay Dharma teachers already teaching in the West.

I began to find my answers when I had an opportunity to meet John at a forty-nine-day Silent Illumination retreat— seven weeks of intensive Chan practice led by Master Sheng Yen. It was very much like the intensives I'd attended at the Chan Center in the past, and I was serving as one of the translators. Six of Master Sheng Yen's most experienced monastics traveled from Taiwan to assist him by conducting teaching interviews and supervising the meditation hall.

My experience shifted when John Crook joined us during the seventh week. When I first met him, I was impressed. He'd spent time in the Himalayas studying with Tibetan yogis and had devoted himself to the serious study of both Zen and Tibetan Buddhism for many years before training with Master Sheng Yen. Not only were John Crook and I both Westerners dedicated to the Chan path, but we were also both trained in the sciences—his fields biology and psychology, mine sociology.

What really touched me was that when I offered to explain to my fellow retreatants what the Chinese words in the texts meant so they could understand what we were reciting in the precepts ceremony where practitioners commit to the ethics of Buddhism, John Crook attended my class! Here was a contemporary of and Dharma heir to my teacher and yet he came to learn from someone like *me*. I was moved by John Crook's manner and how from that moment on he always took the time to give me space and to listen. He treated me as an equal, which wasn't necessarily expected, especially when I was used to a more hierarchical environment.

When asked, "What is the difference between Chinese and non-Chinese students?" Master Sheng Yen once replied, "When you tell Chinese people what to do, they do not challenge the teacher; they do what they are told." This is the outcome of an ethos of Chinese society that emphasizes order and conformity; those who ask questions are often seen as troublemakers, even though all they want is to understand and learn. This is an element of much of Chinese culture and conditioning, and it shows up in all sorts of ways, including a susceptibility to strict regimes.

I grew up in Hong Kong, so of course I understood this, but because I was Western educated—first in British schools and then at American universities—I also knew we each have our own minds and views and can each be our own person. I wanted to know why and how meditation worked, and I had a lot of questions. After all, I was trained in science; I needed a verifiable explanation! That type of inquiry is not always encouraged in a Chinese environment. Even though I was completely committed to Master Sheng Yen as my teacher and was not about to go looking for another, there was a cultural barrier I couldn't break through. Somewhere inside me, I was wondering if I have been going about meditation in the wrong way.

BREAKTHROUGH

A year after our first encounter, John Crook was invited to lead the Western Zen Retreat at Dharma Drum Retreat Center in New York. Developed by John Crook, it was an innovation in Buddhist retreats, offering serious practice in a context more relatable for Westerners.

In the traditional Chan retreats I attended during that time, the monastics discouraged asking a lot of questions. We were instructed to only ask questions related to our meditation practice in our face-to-face interviews with Master Sheng Yen. At this point I was doing fine in my sitting meditation, or so I thought. I had begun my practice using the method of counting the breath and moved on to working with the *huatou* (derived from a koan) method—using a question to focus the mind and reveal emptiness—but would not say that I actually got it. Then, Master Sheng Yen introduced me to the Chan practice of Silent Illumination—as much a way of being as a meditation method. I was good at sitting still and being calm, so I didn't have much to ask in the interviews, but this didn't mean I didn't have questions about suffering, how to penetrate what was going on in my mind, and most important, how meditation was supposed to help me with my life.

That is why there was a bigger piece to my encounter with John Crook than bridging the East-West chasm. It had to do with my meditation practice. Beginning with that first Western Zen Retreat, he showed me that *what I had understood as silence was not silence.* Silence does not mean to push away or avoid all noise; doing that is resisting the present moment and the joy and liberation it holds. Silence means to refrain from succumbing to our habitual reactivity that gets in the way of fully experiencing the present moment as it is. As Master Sheng Yen told John Crook, "Even under the Bodhi tree thought was present. The sutras [Buddhist scriptures] show clearly that the Buddha was aware of his experiences in a way that could be expressed in thought." It was during that retreat that the Dharma teachings I learned from Shifu began to make sense—when Dharma study and practice finally connected—and this book is the product of this coming together of East and West, Dharma study and meditation practice, Chinese Master Sheng Yen and his British Dharma heirs John Crook and Simon Child.

During my work with John in my first Western Zen Retreat, he made it explicit that instead of trying to let go of thought, to stop thinking, or tell myself my thoughts are illusory, it was okay to pay attention to them. *Thoughts are not the enemy; they are just thoughts.* He helped me see how we, perhaps especially as Western-educated people, must make full contact with whatever shows up in the mind—all the thoughts and feelings however intense or frightening they are—to fully appreciate how our minds are truly empty. It is not a matter of being in a removed position or a detached observer where meditation becomes nothing more than labeling thoughts while still inhabiting a place of me versus everything else—othering, self-cherishing, reifying, and spiritual bypassing. Thanks to John, after years of trying to silence my mind and failing to gain insight, I was able to truly meditate for the first time—this was transformative.

In all my study of meditation I'd never heard anyone talk about thoughts in this way before. Even Master Sheng Yen didn't discuss them like that. Having grown up in Hong Kong and practiced Buddhism in the United States, I am more a British-Chinese-American Buddhist than a Chinese one. Maybe there was something that "real" Chinese people understood in the nuances of the language and could get immediately from Master Sheng Yen's teaching, but as a Westerner I'd been missing it until I attended that retreat with John Crook. I felt seen and *allowed* to be seen. John Crook showed me that when it comes to Buddhism, there is much talk about emptiness, yet being willing to investigate our lives at an experiential level is an integral and often overlooked part of our practice.

It is what I teach in retreats and why I wrote this book because most people who are interested in meditation face challenges like mine. Connecting with the reality of emptiness can be tricky. I hope this book will serve as a guide for practitioners to bridge the gap between concept and direct experience. What I do may be a little different from other students of Master

Sheng Yen because I also trained with John Crook and later Simon Child, Master Sheng Yen's second lay Dharma heir who first studied with John Crook. I am a fusion. While I received full Dharma transmission from Simon Child, I want to preserve and acknowledge John Crook's contribution to Chan Buddhism, and Master Sheng Yen will always be my root teacher.

Since that first retreat with John many years ago, I've used what I learned from my teachers to help practitioners recognize how the earnest effort to block out thoughts obstructs them and causes suffering. They can't accept and believe it is okay to allow thoughts to be in the mind as they are, yet they've discovered blocking them out is unsustainable. To help these practitioners get out of their own way, the method I offer to my students is the Chan practice of Silent Illumination.

SILENT ILLUMINATION

Silent Illumination is a way of penetrating the mind through curious inquiry—not elimination. It is a method of reconnecting with our true nature where everything exists and there is no suffering—an especially meaningful, accessible, and portable practice at a time when there is so much complexity, upheaval, and anguish in the world. Like mindfulness and loving-kindness, Silent Illumination is a traditional Buddhist method—actually, the method of no-method. It is simple but quite subtle, and it is meaningful for secular and Buddhist audiences, new and seasoned meditators alike. Those who engage in the Chan practice of Silent Illumination find themselves better able to fully connect with who they are and understand their true nature, developing wisdom and compassion so that they can live more fully for themselves and the world.

Building on the foundations that Master Sheng Yen gave me, John Crook and Simon Child helped me see how this Chan approach to meditation is different from ones where quieting the mind is undertaken first, followed by cultivating insight. With Silent Illumination, still mind and awakening are simultaneous—there is no separation. I stress that it is not "Be silent and you will get illuminated." It is "Illumination comes with silence, from silence, in silence." When John Crook compiled a book of Master Sheng Yen's teachings on Silent Illumination, he titled it *Illuminating Silence*, which I find most useful. It makes the practice active. Silent Illumination is not a step, not a sequence. It is not a thing. It is not a state. It is not first you are silent and then . . . *illumination!* In Chan, it is concurrent—the silence *with* the illumination, the stilling of the mind *with* the awakening. The investigation is like other Buddhist methods; the difference with Chan is the simultaneity.

The Chan practice of Silent Illumination does not take any specific form. For example, while monasteries play an important role in preserving the Buddhist teachings, you do not need to live in a monastery to see the nature of your true self and stop the cycle of suffering. Similarly, being part of a community of practitioners does support and nourish your practice, but you do not need to belong to a Buddhist organization to practice. Anyone—regardless of education level, cultural background, class, gender, race, sexual orientation, religion, physical and intellectual ability, and so on—can practice Chan. To practice Silent Illumination, there are only a few requirements. Cultivating a correct understanding of the Buddha's teachings is crucial. Cultivating a mind that refrains from harming others and works for the benefit of others is essential. You must be motivated. And you need to maintain total clear awareness of the body and mind in this space, moment after moment.

LEGACY

Seven years after Master Sheng Yen passed away, I received Dharma transmission from his disciple and my current teacher Simon Child; I became a full heir in the Chan lineage. It is said that while speaking to a large gathering, Shakyamuni Buddha handed his disciple Mahakasyapa a single flower. He responded to the Buddha's gesture with a subtle smile and in that moment received the first Dharma transmission. Nobody in the crowd knew what was going on, and as they tried to deduce the meaning, Mahakasyapa remained fully present with the Buddha. In that interaction, according to Chan tradition, the Buddha and his disciple understood each other so perfectly that words were unnecessary.

Students, seekers, and scholars have analyzed the story of Mahakasyapa and the Buddha and imagined all the implications of how grasping at conceptual thought to understand the present moment is futile. Conceptual analysis distorts and obscures what enlightenment and Dharma transmission are. The practice of Silent Illumination takes us to this realization.

Enlightenment cannot be expressed in words or evaluated conceptually. Whenever we impose language or thought on an experience, feeling, or phenomena, we are no longer entirely present. Whatever we are talking about is not exactly *it*. This is a truth many people find incredibly mysterious, and therefore the role of the Chan master is to validate and authenticate the enlightenment experience of their students. As Master Sheng Yen pointed out, only someone who has a verified enlightenment experience can confirm it in another. Only someone who has seen the nature of emptiness can understand and relate to the experiential realization of another person. That is what is meant by mind-to-mind transmission in Chan.

So many people misunderstand Dharma transmission as an accomplishment. They think it represents having achieved something or attained a status. That is not an accurate understanding. Master Sheng Yen described Dharma heirs as those who have accepted a heavy responsibility to carry on the lineage—tasked with finding and training the next generation of lineage holders—as custodians of that continuous thread the Buddha passed to Mahakasyapa. A Dharma heir must have a stable personality and a correct understanding of the Buddhist teachings; they must have given rise to Bodhi mind (compassion balanced with wisdom) and made a great vow to share the practice to benefit all sentient beings. Master Sheng Yen taught that lineage transmission means a commitment to making Dharma practice the most important priority in life.

As John Crook showed me, there is a power in being an outsider. Although monasticism is a means of preserving the sanctity of the Dharma, it is not a requirement; the beauty of Chan is that because it is a formless practice, I do not have to refrain from activities like maintaining close ties with family or pursuing a professional career. Living in the world, I have access to and understanding of challenges like emotional relationships, political divisiveness, sexuality, ambition, oppression, and money worries. As a lineage holder yet a lay teacher, my family and my job are not a distraction from practice but rather integral to it. *Life does not get in the way; it is the way.*

Silent Illumination is a perfect vehicle for realizing this because it is such a complete yet portable method. It does not require a retreat. Although concentrated practice can accelerate the learning process and deepen it, it is not required. It is not even necessary for you to be able to do sitting meditation to practice Silent Illumination, although sitting meditation can help settle the mind and maintain contact with the present moment. You can practice while you work, commute, fix meals, attend meetings, play with your children, or wait in line. Wherever you are and whatever you are doing, you can engage in this method of no-method because, as I'll show you in this book, during all of these moments you can uncover deep insight about your mind, yourself, the reality around us, and the true nature of the world. Like Mahakasyapa, you too can remain fully in the present moment, free yourself from the unhelpful habit of suffering, and realize that this moment is perfect as it is and there is nothing missing.

1

THE METHOD OF NO-METHOD
What Silent Illumination Is

Silent Illumination is often called the method of no-method because it does not ask us to focus the mind on any particular object such as the breath. There is nothing to do, but you can't do nothing, so you have to start with something. It is a way of clear and total open awareness, moment-to-moment experience that simultaneously reveals our intrinsic enlightenment. Silent Illumination is a relaxing into the present that allows us to shed our habits of self-centered attachment—and consequently our suffering—without force, like leaves falling from a tree in autumn.

Beautiful words, right? However, you may be thinking, "So, you are telling me to sit here and cultivate clear awareness while seeing my intrinsic enlightenment. But if there is no method, *what am I supposed to do*?"

Good question.

First, it is helpful to understand a little bit about what these two words—*silent* and *illumination*—mean when it comes to

Chan practice. For many people just hearing the words can cause some misunderstanding of what it is that we are doing. It is important to remember that language is limited in its power to accurately describe and articulate what is going on when we meditate, so we need to be very careful not to use our preconceived notions to interpret these terms.

Let's start with the *silent* in Silent Illumination. The word might make you think, "Ah! I know exactly what it is: Blank mind. Silent mind. Nothing-going-on mind." And you may believe you know what to do next: tell yourself to shut up as you try to silence the mind. By doing this, you can make it so that no thought arises, so that everything is completely quiet. You may create the illusion of silence by blocking thoughts from your awareness, but that is not an accurate understanding of "silence" in Silent Illumination.

Silence refers to *nonreactivity* to the activity of our minds—thoughts, feelings, memories, anticipation—rather than the absence of activity itself. To put it another way, silence is about not succumbing to habitual reactivity to what is going on. Of course, as many meditation teachers have said in myriad ways, this is simple but not easy. We each have a living, breathing body with a brain that works and neurons that fire, and as long as we are alive, we will experience sensations and thoughts. That is not a problem; it is not something bad that needs eliminating. It is part of being human. Entrenched within each of us is the habit of creating suffering by activating what Master Sheng Yen called vexations (*klesha*s in Sanskrit). The three most common vexations are as follows:

- Craving more of what we perceive to be pleasant
- Being averse to, hating, or resisting what we perceive to be unpleasant
- Harboring fundamental ignorance or lack of clarity about the true nature of existence—that every moment is the coming together of many causes and conditions, which is often referred to as emptiness (or *shunyata*)

Think about the times you have been in a space where everyone is supposed to be quiet—at a lecture or concert, perhaps in a library. You make a sound, and someone turns to you and says, "Shh! Be quiet." They have not prevented the first sound and have instead made more noise. Imagine it is someone else making the noise, perhaps by dropping a cup. There is a sound and then it is gone. But if we react by saying, "What a terrible sound! Why can't that person be more careful?" that is not silence. It is noise we added. Things happen. Thoughts arise. And then they go away. There is no need to react to them, perpetuate them, or judge them, agitating the mind unnecessarily.

Bring that kind of understanding to your meditation practice. If you are meditating and a thought arises and you tell yourself not to think, to keep quiet, or to shut up, you are making noise and agitating the mind. This is not silence. The thought is there (that is not a problem), but the noise we make in response to the thought is the opposite of the silence of Silent Illumination and comes from our habitual reactivity, no place else.

To look at it another way, you might hear the word *silence* and think, "Oh, silence means nothing. Nothing in the mind.

How do I get rid of everything?" This is an extremely common response, this attachment to quietism. If you have that tendency, be conscious of it. Allow yourself to be clearly aware, fully experiencing whatever is going on, whatever is arising in your mind. Silence does not mean nothing is happening in the mind. Silence refers to knowing clearly what is arising there but not succumbing to the compulsion to push it away, crave more of it, block it, or deny its presence. Those are all types of mental agitation; they are not silence.

The Chinese words for Silent Illumination can also be translated as "serene clarity." It is a helpful choice of words because *serene* does not immediately imply no sound, which tends to be the automatic association most of us make with the word *silence*. The word *serene* evokes tranquil, calm, unflustered, or unagitated. *Letting be.* For example, seeing thoughts and allowing them rather than pushing them away. Think of Silent Illumination as this practice of allowing. We can be serene about what is going on and clearly aware that there are thoughts. We needn't fall into our compulsion to push them away or act on them; instead, we can allow the thought to be here—fully seen, heard, and experienced—and move on.

Silent Illumination is not about engaging in meditation with the hope that nothing challenging will happen in life. That is wishful thinking. Some people get stuck there as if believing they've found some secret deal we can make with the Buddha promising that nothing bad will happen if we meditate in just the right way. We won't lose our jobs, our parents won't die, our kids will get perfect grades in school— whatever we think is our perfect life. When difficult things happen, we feel that all our practice was for nothing. Check to see if you secretly harbor such beliefs. They can operate without our knowing it.

As John Crook showed me, silence does not mean that nothing happens in the mind. In fact, during meditation, whether it is sitting meditation or moving practice, powerful emotions can arise. You can be fully with whatever is in your mind, experiencing it all the way from the moment it emerges to the moment it fades to nothing, but usually that is not how we experience emotions. Maybe we feel sadness and think, "I do not want to feel that. I am strong. I am not supposed to feel sad." Or we feel anger and think, "I am not supposed to feel angry. I've been taught that we are not supposed to feel angry."

That is not silence.

When an emotion arises in response to something that happened, that is a mental sensation and through the practice of Silent Illumination you can learn to notice it and allow it to go away effortlessly. (Remember those leaves falling from the tree?) What happens is that our reaction or resistance, coming from our conditioning—very often cultural conditioning—leads us to automatically assume some inherently good or bad qualities about each sensation that compels us to react, adding judgmental thoughts—and that is not silence. This nonsilence—this agitation of the mind—blocks our ability to clearly see and realize the true nature of reality, the true nature of our self as it is. You might have read or heard podcasts, talks, and books describing this, but only you can access it in this moment.

Reality as it is. It is all here. That is illumination.

Illumination and silence are not separate. Silent Illumination is not a sequence. It is not "I'll become silent first and then illumination will happen." Silence and illumination are two sides of the same coin, illumination being the function of a mind that is not reactive. As we practice, we'll come to experience illumination of everything as it is—connected, not separate. It is merely our idea that there is this and that, there is me and you, and even there is silence and there is illumination. This creates a distorted view and blocks us from seeing that everything is the manifestation of the coming together of many causes and conditions: we are all interconnected.

Think about what you are doing right now. You are focusing on these words and perhaps trying to figure out what I am saying. This is a convergence of moments—our learning to read and write, everything and everyone involved in the publication and distribution of this book, your choice of this book among all the others on the shelf, the circumstances in your life that allow you to have this moment to sit down to read. This moment is a miracle cocreated by all of this and all of us. You may stay with my words and decide to give this practice a try and allow it to transform your life, but you could as easily succumb to another thought like "I'll just watch TV. That is what I usually do in the evening to relax." You can follow that thought, put down the book, never return to it, and the practice of Silent Illumination will not become part of your life. Every moment, every thought and action in response to those thoughts, shapes future moments that together make up our lives. Yet we are seldom aware of the fact that we hold the key to reveal the true nature of our own lives right now in this moment.

We tend not to understand our self and reality this way. We believe, "I made this happen. It is all me and me alone, fighting against the obstacles thrown at me by the world." I would be mistaken to think that I wrote this book. The reality is we all wrote this book together. Your desire for spiritual growth is one of the causes and conditions that got publishers, editors, and booksellers interested in this endeavor. Without my teachers and the practitioners in my Dharma classes and Chan retreats, there would be nothing for me to share on these pages. I did my part in initiating the project and carrying it through, but it would be a huge distortion of reality to think that "I" made this happen. Without the encouragement and support of everyone involved, directly or indirectly, and all the institutions in our society that make it possible for an ordinary person like me to write and publish a book, you would not be reading this. If I believe that I made this book happen through my own hard work and intellect it becomes all about me, and that is not the whole reality. Yet, subtly, one way or another, we all forget this, and when we do, we obstruct the Silent Illumination that reveals the true nature of our reality.

WE CREATE OUR SUFFERING

So, what is the point of all this?

Why not put down this book and go watch television?

Why sit in meditation doing nothing for any amount of time?

Why bother with Silent Illumination?

What does it have to do with my life?

Are you asking these questions? I hope so! This kind of inquiry is important because it is easy to engage in a practice and just do it and forget what it is that we are doing and why.

Here's the short answer: we practice Silent Illumination to end suffering—ours and everyone else's. I'll go into a lot more detail throughout the book, especially when I talk about the

Buddha's very first sermon on the Four Noble Truths, but for now remember: our habitual and often default ways of thinking and reacting cause us to suffer. Most of the time, no matter what is going on, we want something different, we want something else. Many of us may have experienced this when taking a vacation. We plan our trip for months and look forward to being in a new setting where we can finally relax and be happy and away from the stress at work and home. After the initial excitement of arriving in a new place, we may begin to notice flaws with the food or the bed or the service at the hotel. We find ourselves missing our familiar food and routine. Even if we enjoy the trip, the final days are spent dreading the return to work and stressing about the overfilled email inbox awaiting us. We arrive home upset about the vacation not quite meeting our expectations; we do not feel as happy or as satisfied as we thought we would.

Here's another example: My nephews love to play video games. Their mom controls their screen time and limits how much they play each day. I have often watched them laughing and having fun while they played for the thirty minutes they were given. When their time was almost up, they begged for more. When the Wi-Fi was turned off, their faces showed their dissatisfaction and frustration. All the joy and happiness they had experienced moments earlier was completely forgotten. There was only suffering.

All of this is the opposite of happiness, contentment, equanimity, or wisdom. Silent Illumination helps us realize that suffering is not our true nature. If we allow it, contentment is our natural state of being. The practice of Silent Illumination allows us to reconnect with our birthright, a state we experience as deep inner peace, joy, unconditional love, clarity, flow, and full connection.

In fact, what we experience as suffering is conditioned, meaning that it is the coming together of what is happening and our reaction to what is happening. As I have mentioned, we have a body and mind, so we will have sensations, thoughts, feelings—that is part of being human. There is nothing wrong with that, and we are not trying to engage in Silent Illumination practice so that we do not feel anything.

Think about it. Are we going to stop being human? Wouldn't it be strange if a loved one passed away and you didn't feel anything? It's perfectly natural to feel sad when we are faced with someone's death. You are being human because you are capable of loving someone and therefore you will experience the sadness of separation. But does that mean that you necessarily have to suffer from the experience of sadness? *No.*

The arising of sadness upon separation is natural, but it is not permanent. When the situation changes, it goes away. You may feel an intense sorrow and then it fades. Where it becomes suffering is when we tell ourselves, "I am not supposed to be sad" or believe that "This sadness will permanently define my life from now on." We may be worried that if we allow the sadness to arise, we will be paralyzed by grief, will never stop being sad. These are habitual thoughts that turn the experience of sadness into a fixed entity. We aren't practicing Silent Illumination when we repress a feeling and forbid ourselves to connect with our naturally arising human emotions. Through the practice of Silent Illumination, we can allow ourselves to fully experience sadness, or any emotion, and when fully experienced, it will be discharged. There is no need to believe in an abstract idea that these emotions are impermanent. We directly experience them as such.

It is the same thing with anger. It is upsetting when we see ourselves or others treated unfairly because of race, gender, class, sexual orientation, religion, or other differences. We feel angry thoughts arising. When we allow ourselves to experience these thoughts fully by staying with their unfolding, we maintain the clear awareness of each emerging present moment. These may be strong emotions accompanied by powerful compulsions to act in hurtful ways. If we stay with them, we will notice they are discharged when fully acknowledged and accepted, and their intensity fades, so we can see the entire situation more clearly and know how best to respond. The angry feelings and thoughts that arise in response to an upsetting situation are normal and transient. We turn them into suffering when we try to convince ourselves that a situation should not bother us, or we tell ourselves that we are not angry when angry thoughts are already part of the present moment. Often, we are angry that we have angry thoughts. Without clear awareness, we perpetuate these thoughts by being angry that we got angry at having angry thoughts. With the practice of Silent Illumination, we can recognize the complex feelings and thoughts unfolding in the present moment and give them space. By doing so, we are less likely to react compulsively and can find the clarity and courage to do what is needed and appropriate in each moment.

Consider fear. During the early days and weeks of the coronavirus outbreak, many of us experienced intense fear. We found ourselves in very real danger of dying from a new disease and losing our livelihood because of a rapidly deteriorating economy. It is natural for fear to arise in the face of such intense threats to our survival. It serves as an alarm to focus our mind and be vigilant. At that time, I was holding weekly sessions to support a group of Chan practitioners. As they stayed with the practice, they reported feeling less anxious as the weeks went by and we learned more about the virus and appropriate measures to slow its spread. The fear served its function of directing us to pay attention to the necessary precautions to stay safe during the outbreak. We can still be careful but not be paralyzed by irrational fear. Often, instead of seeing fear for what it is—a smoke alarm that turns off when the danger of fire has passed—and being thankful that the alarm works, we develop an aversion to our fear or identify with it as the essence of our being. *This is suffering.*

THE COMING TOGETHER OF EXPERIENCE AND VEXATIONS

The practice of Silent Illumination allows us to see the myriad ways in which we generate our own suffering and gives us the opportunity to unlearn these unhelpful habits. Equating emotion with suffering is problematic—the first is an experience and the second a reaction. To better understand this, I find Master Sheng Yen's approach particularly insightful. He spoke about suffering as the coming together of the present moment and vexations.

We'll go into more depth when we get into the subtle habits of the mind I call the "modes of operation," but for now remember: the present moment + vexation = suffering. This means that when we neither react to what is happening nor stay entrenched in the habit of objectifying what is going on in our lives, there is no suffering. What is happening is just what is happening. For example, I am at my desk writing these words. There is some soreness in my lower back. This sensation is a normal part of having a body and sitting for an extended period of time. Thanks to nerve cells that are working properly, signals are reaching my brain so that I am aware of the soreness. There is no problem. Yet, if I let the habit of generating vexations take over when I am not paying attention to the unfolding present moment, I'd label the sensation as an enemy, perceive it as waging a war against me, and react by hating it and fighting against it. I'd try to get rid of it and in the process tense up my body and mind and end up in more pain. This is a common reaction for practitioners of meditation when they experience physical discomfort. When it happens, it is a great opportunity to observe how habituated we are at creating suffering by adding vexation to the present-moment experience.

Once we see the pattern, we can apply it to everything in our lives. That is the conceptual understanding of Silent Illumination, but the *practice* of it is about realizing it, allowing what is to be as it is. It is about being with what is, wholly, without giving rise to vexations. The moment we remember to practice this way, there is no suffering. It is not magic—it is the law of causes and conditions. Because suffering is the coming together of the present moment and vexations, when vexations do not arise, there is no suffering.

As you will see in this book, we are very much entrenched in the habitual tendencies that give rise to vexations—the modes of operation. That is our habit; we are unable to do as the Chinese Song dynasty Chan Master Hongzhi (1091–1175) advised: "Stay with that just as that. Stay with this just as this."

You might find these words useful, almost as a mantra for your practice: "Stay with that just as that. Stay with this just as this." Nothing more. And it is not "Oh, this meditation is really good. I am really calm. I want it to be *calmer*." It is just this. *It is this.* And stay with this just as this. Maybe you have a busy mind with a lot of thoughts coming through. Be with the busy mind. Stay with that just as that, without trying to get rid of or silence any thought.

That is the teaching of Silent Illumination. We find it quite difficult because we are habituated to do the opposite. *Anything* but stay with this just as this. So how do we do it?

ENTERING THE PRACTICE OF SILENT ILLUMINATION

Because Silent Illumination is not a method per se, but a natural state of being, learning to practice it is about recognizing our habits of getting in the way of this natural state and unlearning those unhelpful habits. However, there are steps we can take to get closer to that natural state while sitting in meditation, and these begin with Silent Illumination as a practice of just sitting.

Begin by finding a posture for the body to sit in a way that is stable and relatively comfortable, allowing yourself to relax into the posture. Relaxing the entire body is important in your meditation, beginning at the top of your head all the way down to your toes, allowing your body to settle into its posture, minimizing tension in your muscles, and allowing the mind to mirror this and settle down as well.

Do that for a moment—simply sit and fully enjoy and experience your body and mind right here, right now. This is the practice of just sitting.

As your mind becomes more settled, you can appreciate that there are no new stimuli from your life—you are not at your desk, your computer is off, you are not engaging with people or doing activities—and consequently fewer and fewer fresh stories, thoughts, or information come in. As your mind settles, continue to practice just sitting. As you allow your body and mind to settle, cultivate a total clear awareness of the moment-to-moment experience of this body-mind sitting in this space. As you do this, habitual tendencies will reveal themselves, arising in your mind as a succession of thoughts and actions. There is nothing inevitable about the outcome, as you can always choose to stop giving rise to the next thought in the familiar plot. With this clear awareness, you practice remembering that there is nothing permanent and inevitable in the unfolding present moment. Seeing these habitual tendencies as they really are—a succession of thoughts and actions that are allowed to take over your mind when you are not paying attention—you can unlearn the unhelpful habit of reacting with vexations by not perpetuating well-established thought patterns. You practice Silent Illumination by allowing whatever is in the present moment to be, while maintaining and cultivating clear awareness and recognizing and releasing the compulsive habitual reactivity again and again to fully experience each unfolding present moment as it is.

It is easy to describe but less easy to do.

In this "just sitting" practice, along with the changing sensations of the body, we cultivate clear awareness of everything that comes through our mind. I invite you to do this. Notice your mind's reactions, particularly the drifting that occurs in the present moment. When you see that your mind has drifted, you haven't made a mistake or failed meditation—that noticing is part of clear awareness. When you notice that you are frustrated because your mind has drifted off the method, *that* is part of clear awareness. When you notice that you are trying to get rid of your thoughts, *that* is part of clear awareness.

Sit with this allowing of total clear awareness for a moment.

LET THROUGH, LET BE, LET GO

Both John Crook and Simon Child have taught this process as "let through, let be, let go." "Letting through" means allowing everything that arises in the present moment to cross the mind. We have strong opinions about what should not be allowed in the present moment and want to block it. Doing so tenses up and agitates the mind. More importantly, it is foolish to try to block thoughts because they are already part of the present moment. Let them through by releasing the compulsion to push them out. Allowing also does not mean inviting or following thoughts. We are not saying, "Hey, what is going on? How are things with my family? What were the headlines this morning? Why do my knees hurt?" As we practice, we do not go out of our way to find mental stimulation. Notice the habit to seek out mental stimulation, believing that you have to fill your mind with thoughts the way we fill our homes with stuff or our schedules with activities. When you hear a sound—someone coughs, the refrigerator hums, a car door slams—or you feel a sensation like a tickle on your nose, or a memory comes up like your mom talking to you, allow that sound, sensation, recollection, or whatever it is to come through your mind as it is. *Try this.*

As you let thoughts through, maintain clear awareness of the moment-to-moment experience of the body and mind sitting in this space. Notice the habits of not wanting to let some thoughts through like "Thoughts, you are not welcome. I want to keep my mind pure. I do not want to let unpleasant memories or uncomfortable sensations come in. You are not welcome!" Remember, like it or not, these thoughts are already in your mind when you notice them. You might as well let them come through instead of blocking them, which will only tense up the mind. The blocking and denial of entry generates agitation in the mind. That is not silence. There is no need to busy ourselves with blocking them out; simply see the thoughts for what they are: the coming together of constantly changing causes and conditions, no different from the sounds of the birds or cars outside the window. It is okay to let thoughts through because we know that whatever arises in the mind can come through and depart. *Sit for a moment as whatever arises comes through.*

Letting whatever arises come through your mind doesn't mean looking for thoughts or manufacturing them. We do not come to meditation with a to-do list. The second element of this sitting practice is to *allow* whatever comes through your mind *to be*. Let it all be as it is. Some of these thoughts, feelings, or sensations arise and are gone in an instant. It is a flicker, so allow it to go. You may notice thoughts like "That feeling is really good. I like this thought!" arising. It's not a problem. See the thoughts for what they are, just thoughts, no different from bubbles that form and burst. You do not have to believe in them or act them out. You may feel the urge to hold on to the pleasant thought. That, too, is part of the emerging present moment. Allow it to arise and depart on its own.

Some thoughts are more than a flicker, and they linger. Perhaps there is a memory or a fantasy. Notice the habit of wanting to hold on to it or make it go away. Allow it to be fully experienced, felt, and seen. You may assume that you already know it since it is a memory. The recalling of the memory is happening in the present. How does it feel to be recalling this event in this brand-new moment? If a similar thought or memory shows up again, be fully present with it. Pay full attention and you may notice something you have overlooked. Be curious and cultivate the beginner's mind. Allow the story to unfold without engaging with it and trust that it will go away on its own because nothing stays in the mind forever . . . nothing. In fact, the more you resist the things that linger in your mind and the more you try to get rid of them, the more power you are giving them and the more likely they are to return. *Give this a try and see for yourself.*

Sitting, letting through, and allowing to be . . . these are all about unlearning our usual way of reacting. When we respond with "I do not like this feeling. I want to get rid of it" or "I'll allow this thought to be for three seconds . . . okay, time's up. Out!" we are placing restrictions or creating rules that are not necessary, and that is not letting be. It is not silence. Imagine you have a house in the wilderness with a big backyard. Cats wander in and hang out. Groundhogs wander in . . . deer . . . bear. If you confront them or try to confine them, you are causing yourself unnecessary stress; however, if you allow them to look around and nibble on a little something, let them do what wildlife does, they will leave on their own. You can just enjoy living in the wilderness. You know they are there, and you recognize what they are doing without reacting, and you are also aware of how their presence makes you feel. This is letting through, letting be.

As you allow yourself to fully experience everything in its complexity without labels like "These thoughts feel sad and painful" or "This story makes me so happy," notice how, when these thoughts of labeling and commenting take over, we are disconnected from the next emerging present moment. When we substitute concepts and labels for direct experience, we miss the nuances of our actual experience. Notice the urge to label. It's not a problem. Gently stay with the moment-to-moment experience of being here. Let the contents of the mind and the labels pass through. Allow yourself to directly experience the unfolding present moment and as mental activity fades, allow it to fade. There is no need to follow it. Letting go is to allow it to go on its own.

Notice our tendency to be in a hurry to make thoughts go away, especially for those deemed unacceptable. That is not letting go. The difference is in our attitude. If it stays, it's fine. If it goes, it's fine. We are fully present, allowing whatever comes through the mind to be fully experienced, moment after moment. Do not confuse this with dissociating; we are fully engaged with life as it is as we sit with this body and mind in this space. If it stays, it stays; if it goes, it goes. No problem. There is no need to add, judge, cling, or perpetuate.

And as you let through, let be, and let go, you are practicing just sitting, fully experiencing whatever passes through your mind in each unfolding present moment. That means experiencing everything, including all sensations, thoughts, feelings, stories, and your resistance to them—everything. Do not expect to be able to do this instantly. Gradually, as you practice, you will begin to see which habits, or modes of operation, you are particularly attached to and will begin to learn something about how your mind works.

RELAXING INTO REALITY AS IT IS

How do we know the mind is settling down and the entrenched habitual tendencies are being activated less often? As the body and mind settle and relax into the present moment, they are more unified. The burden of the body disappears as the mind merges with the moment-to-moment experience of bodily sensations. As the mind settles, the entrenched habit of pitting body/mind against the external world is not activated. We feel unified with the surrounding environment as the wall we built in our mind around our skin dissolves. The usual sense of conflict with the outside world pauses and rests. We are completely at ease just being here. As we continue to cultivate this total clear awareness that encompasses everything, we can experience a vast boundlessness both internally and externally, unimpeded.

Remember, words like *body*, *mind*, and *environment* divide our practice into three different parts, but they are really all one. Until we cultivate total clear awareness, we tend to experience mind, body, and the environment as if they are separate entities. When we allow the body/mind in this space to be fully experienced as it is, moment to moment, there is a clear knowing that body, mind, and environment are really one. This knowing is experiential, not conceptual.

As you practice relaxing into each emerging present moment, you might experience the boundary between the body and mind fading, softening, dissolving. You might notice bodily sensations of your thoughts and emotions. You might experience parts of your body tensing up as your mind becomes agitated by the habit of grasping or rejecting. Those moments allow you to see how this division between body and mind is arbitrary, conceptual. We give the body and mind names, but we experience them as one *if* we allow ourselves to do so without attaching to the arbitrary boundaries that we have created by holding on to an idea that they are separate. That is why Master Hongzhi taught that we should fully experience everything without objectifying it, meaning without turning *this* into something separate from *that*. It is all here—body and mind.

As you sit, you might also feel the boundary between body and mind and *environment* is fading. Perhaps you hear the sound of a car driving by, but you feel like it is happening inside you. That is when body, mind, and environment are unified. No separation. When we live in the world, we hold on to this boundary that is built between our body and the outside world, between you and me, inside and outside. The practice of Silent Illumination dissolves this sense of separation that is held in place with tension in our mind, and allows the mind to return to its natural expansive state. You can reconnect with how our whole being is truly interconnected with everything.

Where does the outside end and the inside begin? This idea that there is an inside and an outside separated by a solid boundary is created by the mind. When we allow ourselves to just be here, to let through, let be, let go, we experience reality as it is. Everything is here. There is no need for these words creating these boundaries. The body, mind, and environment unify. The tension generated to reify the boundaries between this and that, inside and outside, melts away. In this stillness, the entrenched habit of suffering can be illuminated and released.

This practice of Silent Illumination has transformed my life. I used to suffer a lot and was too ignorant to even know I was suffering. I simply felt closed in and imprisoned by what I did not know. I was desperate to break free but had no idea how. Life was a struggle even though my basic needs were met, my work was going well, and my family was loving. It was maddening as there was nothing obvious to blame for my unhappiness. Silent Illumination shed light on the many ways I have caused suffering for myself and others. This recognition allowed and continues to allow me to take responsibility for my past actions and frees me from the burden and dread of my past. It lets me see clearly how habits of vexation are perpetuated and gives me confidence that I can unlearn unhelpful and destructive mental patterns I picked up unwittingly as I moved through life. The process is ongoing, but I now know what to do when vexations arise and suffering results. It is all part of being human. It is not a problem.

The key is remembering to reconnect with our natural state of being when we fall into the habit of suffering. That natural state of being is Silent Illumination. The practice is simple but not easy. Oftentimes the best way to understand the practice is to understand what it is *not*.

2

A DIFFERENT WAY OF BEING
Allowing All to Be Illuminated

"Silently and serenely, one forgets all words. Clearly and vividly, it appears before you." These are the opening lines of Chan Master Hongzhi's poem "Silent Illumination."[3] He was pointing to freedom from suffering, clearly seeing and embracing the interconnectedness of all things and the compassion that naturally arises from this realization. The moment we just allow the present moment to be while being fully present, without succumbing to the habits of objectifying the present moment, craving, and aversion—there is no suffering. We are in Silent Illumination. It is not a state of nothingness. Everything exists; the dynamic coming together of causes and conditions of each emerging present moment is clearly revealed.

When we see clearly that the separation between self and others is an idea and not reality, benefiting others becomes no different from benefiting ourselves. In one sentence, Master Hongzhi showed us how to be free from suffering and how we are habituated to getting in the way of our liberation. This means whether we suffer or not is up to us. Realizing this is profoundly liberating and empowering. We can be in Silent Illumination right now—just stop and drop the entrenched habit of reacting with vexations. Chances are you'll notice that you're not at ease, that you do not even know that your mind is either craving or rejecting, and that you're resisting the idea of not reacting. You may think, "What will happen if my mind stops doing what it does?" *Try it.* You may find yourself freed to be fully here, allowing everything in the moment to be as it is. The entrenched habit of feeling that something is not how it's supposed to be in the present is not activated. It's a different way of being.

Silent Illumination is the natural state of being fully human. There is no need to look outside of ourselves to achieve it. It is already here, within each one of us. We just need to wake up and see it, to reconnect with what is already within us at this very moment. This is why the meditation practice in Silent Illumination is called "just sitting." The method is to abide nowhere and allow the mind to arise, as instructed by Master Huineng (638–713 C.E.), the sixth lineage master in Chan.

In the Tathagatagarbha Sutra there is a story of a boy whose parents sewed a priceless pearl inside his coat. Yet, the boy forgot all about it and as he grew older looked for wealth everywhere. Finding none, he could barely survive. All the while he was in possession of a priceless pearl that he could use to benefit all beings. The pearl in the story refers to our buddha-nature—our natural capacity for wisdom and compassion. It is our capacity to see clearly and act with an appropriate response according to conditions, to see the interconnectedness of all beings, and to love them unconditionally as we see clearly that loving others is no different from loving ourselves. In other words, we each have an innate capacity for wisdom and compassion. We are already fully endowed with this capacity; we are each in possession of this priceless pearl. However, our untrained mind is often too confused and agitated to see this fact and instead we keep looking outward, grasping for what we already possess. This is why Buddhist practice, especially Chan, often involves some form of meditation to train and stabilize the mind to cultivate clarity about how much we get in the way of ourselves.

Meditation in the practice of Silent Illumination is a different way of meditating. For practitioners who started with a method involving a clear object of the mind, such as the breath or counting the breath, it is helpful to understand the difference. Otherwise, you may be inadvertently perpetuating or even strengthening the habits that block you from reconnecting with your buddha-nature instead of unlearning them.

Meditation using the breath to stabilize the mind can help us transition into the practice of Silent Illumination. Since we must breathe to live, the direct experience of the changing sensations of the body with each inhalation and exhalation is a good anchor for maintaining contact with each emerging present moment. We allow the body to breathe naturally, fully experiencing the subtle changing sensations as the diaphragm expands and contracts, air coming in and out of the nostrils, the simple experience of being alive and sitting fully being a breathing body in this space.

As you do this, you will likely notice your mind drifting off, losing contact with the direct experience of the body breathing. It's not a problem. Make use of that as an opportunity to practice remembering to come back to the direct experience of the changing sensations of the body breathing. There is no need to get frustrated when the mind drifts. Setting the breath as the object to rest the mind allows us to be aware of the movement of the mind. It allows us to notice that the mind, like the body, is not fixed; it's constantly changing. So, when you notice the mind drifting off, that noticing is awareness. This clarity allows you to choose to bring your attention back to the breath. It doesn't matter how often the mind drifts; as long as you find your way back to the changing sensations of the body breathing, you are practicing well. When we practice with the breath method this way, the mind settles down.

We can think of the confused and agitated mind like a jar of muddy water. Our habitual tendencies of reacting to the present moment by craving or aversion are movements that shake up the mind, stirring the silt in this jar of water. Resting our attention gently on the changing sensations of the body breathing, moment after moment, is like holding the jar still and allowing the silt to settle on its own. There is no need to do anything to adjust what we believe is disturbing the mind. This only agitates the mind further, like shaking up the jar and stirring up the silt again. As the mind settles, we can see into it more clearly and notice what is going on—the subtle and not-so-subtle ways in which we suffer and cause our suffering.

It is important to correctly understand the function of the breath in stabilizing the mind while cultivating clear awareness of the mind's habitual tendencies. This can be a tricky transition for practitioners who have been using the breath to concentrate the mind. They are used to focusing on the breath by blocking everything else out. It is a narrowing of our attention to a small area such as the nostrils to focus on the breath. This is an effective way to strengthen concentration, and we are familiar with focusing the mind this way. It is like when we focus on a task, such as working on an essay, by blocking out everything else. You can be oblivious to the fact that the sun has set or that you're hungry. The mind tenses up to narrow its focus in this highly concentrated state, and that's why we get quite tired after a while. It is not sustainable to focus the mind in this manner for long periods of time.

With Silent Illumination, we can be fully present and constantly engaged with each task at hand with clarity because Silent Illumination does not involve tensing the mind. Meditating in Silent Illumination is about opening this clear awareness to allow all to be illuminated. When we tense the mind to focus on a narrow area where the breath is felt, we are not allowing the rest of the body, thoughts and emotions, and the environment into our awareness.

To transition into meditating in Silent Illumination, we relax into each emerging present moment, opening our awareness and allowing thoughts and sounds in the environment to be there. For practitioners accustomed to cultivating a highly concentrated mind, this may feel like they have lost their practice. In fact, many practitioners have resisted the instruction to open their awareness because they were convinced that concentrating the mind on only the breath is the right practice. Being able to concentrate is a handy skill, and it can be quite enjoyable to experience the sensations of a concentrated mind in meditation. Training the mind only in this way, however, will not cultivate clear awareness of how we cause suffering to ourselves and others so that we can unlearn these entrenched habits. Concentration alone will not free us from suffering.

Without clarity on our entrenched habits that cause suffering to ourselves and others, we are prone to perpetuate these habits further. Someone who has the habit of being critical, for instance, can become meaner and nastier without being aware of it. Hence, it is helpful to learn to work with the breath method in a gentle way. Instead of holding on to the breath tightly to concentrate the mind by blocking out everything, all we need to do is gently maintain contact with the changing sensations of the body breathing moment after moment. In this way, we are cultivating clear awareness of the entire body. By letting thoughts through, letting them be, and letting them go on their own, we are also cultivating clear awareness of subtle activities in the mind. By allowing sensations such as sound and touch to be experienced fully, we are allowing the environment, such as a car passing by or the room warming up, into our awareness, and thus we allow everything to coexist in each emerging present moment. Practicing this way, the mind can truly settle and become quite still.

THE METHOD OF NO-METHOD

Silent Illumination is called the method of no-method because we are not directing our attention to any object in particular. It is to be fully here, with this body and mind in this space, with total clear awareness moment after moment. Practitioners who start with directing their attention to a small part of the body to focus on the breath often misinterpret the instruction to open their awareness to the body by moving their focused attention around to scan different parts of the body. It's like pointing a searchlight from head to toe. This is not Silent Illumination; this is moving the object of meditation from one part of the body to another. Not surprisingly, practitioners often find that their mind is not settling down and may become more scattered. It is an incorrect understanding of cultivating body awareness. All we need to do is to be mindful that we are sitting here with this body in this space, moment after moment. Remember, we are cultivating total clear awareness of body, mind, *and* the environment. If you are directing your attention to the bodily sensations only, ignoring thoughts and what is going on outside of you, that is not the practice of Silent Illumination.

There are practitioners who might interpret the practice as directing attention to the mind—watching mental activities intensely, resulting in a kind of hypervigilance of thoughts and emotions. This hypervigilance can generate a lot of tension. And oftentimes the focus is stuck on the activities of the mind, forgetting awareness of the body. This intense inward gaze of focusing on the thoughts and emotions takes place at the expense of total clear awareness of the body and surroundings. The tension agitates the mind and is antithetical to settling into clear awareness. One can become quite self-absorbed by focusing so exclusively on thoughts and feelings. That is not the practice of Silent Illumination. Remember, the practice is to open our awareness to include body and mind and the environment simultaneously.

When some practitioners cultivate clear awareness of the body and mind, they dull their awareness of the environment. It is a bit like muffling the sound around us to pay attention to physical sensations and thoughts. In so doing, they are strengthening the mentally constructed boundary that separates self from other. Instead of cultivating clear awareness of interconnectedness with all, they make the separation more pronounced. Practitioners who practice this way report that they feel quite lonely and isolated from others. It's not surprising. They are thickening the wall of the bubble that we are already habituated to hold around us. This is why the practice is to open our awareness to include our surroundings, allowing us to directly experience the unceasing interactions between the body, mind, and environment and in doing so realize that this wall between us and the world is an illusion.

Yet other practitioners might interpret the instruction to open their awareness to include their environment as an instruction to direct their attention outward. They end up becoming acutely aware of bird songs and car alarms while forgetting the awareness of the body and mind. This is not Silent Illumination.

What is common in all these different ways of misinterpreting the instructions is that you are directing the mind toward a certain object—environment, bodily sensations, thoughts, and/or emotions. It is not necessary to busy ourselves with all the directing. We can remain clearly aware, fully experiencing the body and mind sitting here in this space moment after moment without directing attention in any specific way. It's like the difference between pointing a spotlight in the dark only at the body, the mind, the body/mind, or then the environment, and just switching on the light and illuminating the entire space. Because most of us are so habituated to directing our attention to an object and turning it into a method to focus the mind in meditation, it may take some getting used to as you unlearn the habit of directing your mind to an object.

Practicing with the method of no-method is a different way of meditating. As you find your way to the method of no-method, you will discover all the different ways you are *not* allowing the emerging present moment to be. As you shall see, this is how we create suffering for ourselves with our entrenched habits of resisting the present moment.

CALMING THE MIND VERSUS MAKING THE MIND CALM

It is helpful to distinguish between "calming the mind" and "making the mind calm" and to avoid doing the latter in meditation. "Calming the mind" is allowing the mind to settle naturally by gently maintaining contact with each emerging present moment facilitated by using an anchor such as the changing sensations of the body breathing. As the mind settles, subtle thought patterns are clearly seen, allowing us to stop perpetuating them.

"Making the mind calm" involves forcing the issue, not letting things happen in the mind, not letting yourself feel something like anxiety or fear. If we are worried about a sick family member or anxious about a precarious situation at work, asking ourselves to not feel worried is unhelpful. It is normal to experience emotions when we go through the ups and downs in our lives. Instead, when you meditate, if you notice worry or anxiety arising, experience them fully, allow them to be seen, heard, and felt, recognizing that it is natural for fear to arise when we are in an uncertain situation. When we allow the anxiety through and fully experience it, we see that what is labeled "anxiety" constantly changes; the bodily sensations and thoughts and feelings of the experience ebb and flow, arising and perishing. We can see that no reaction is a permanent part of us; it is part of the flow of each emerging present moment.

It is easier to see this in terms of other people. When someone is anxious and very worried, you might tell them worrying doesn't help anything and suggest they calm down. That is not going to calm their mind. It is going to increase the agitation. Imagine the mind like a tranquil lake—sometimes a breeze causes ripples in the water. That is normal. The ripples are not a permanent characteristic of the lake but a coming together of causes and conditions—air moving and touching the surface of water in liquid state (if the lake is frozen, a breeze won't cause ripples). If we try to stop those ripples by pressing them down with our hand, we are not going to calm the water; we will create more agitation and bigger ripples. The more we try to make the water calm by smoothing out the ripples, the more agitation we create.

The same applies to our minds—they can't be made calm by suppressing or blocking thoughts or pushing them out. Rather, when we practice Silent Illumination, we are fully there—*stay with that just as that*—relaxing into each emerging present moment, moment after moment after moment. . . . When thoughts arise, they are not your enemy; they are not a problem.

Allow thoughts to be there. Truly and unconditionally allow them to be there. Notice your tendency to set all kinds of conditions and restrictions on the present moment and how you tense up the mind in the process. Even by saying, "You can be here but only for a little while," you are not letting the thoughts be and will be in a hurry to push them out when the time you have allotted for the thought has ended. It is our way of pressing down the ripples on the water, trying to *make* the mind calm.

Calming the mind, on the other hand, is when you simply allow your thoughts to be there, fully felt and heard, with no limit set before the thoughts must go. It is as if a small child has just woken up from a nightmare and is terrified, crying, and very upset. What would you do? Tell the child to shut up and calm down? Or tell the child that you will hold her for one minute and then she must shut up? Of course not! Chances are the child will get more upset. The same applies to our mind. Making our mind calm or making our mind anything but just mind as it is, is not Silent Illumination.

Silent Illumination is also not about trying to make the mind calm by eliminating the unpleasant aspects of whatever may be going on. Instead, you continuously stay with what is going on with clarity. Practicing this way, we are being truly kind to ourselves and cultivating the habit of being unconditionally compassionate to everyone we encounter. As we do this, we find and cultivate this clarity of what current causes and conditions allow us to do and what we can do to cultivate the conditions to make the change that we would like to see. It is not passive; it is fully engaged.

If we are not trying to make the mind calm, how do we know if we are practicing properly? If we are letting thoughts through, how do we know we are not just sitting there day-dreaming? As we cultivate total clear awareness, allowing ourselves to just be, the mind can become quite still. Simon Child likes to use this quote by Master Hongzhi to describe the stillness in Silent Illumination as we keep relaxing into and embracing the totality of each emerging present moment:

Your body should sit silently; your mind should be quiescent and unmoving; and your mouth, so still that moss grows around it and grasses sprout from your tongue. Do this without cease, cleansing the mind until it gains the clarity of an autumn pool and is as bright as the moon illuminating the autumn sky.[4]

"Quiescent" here does not mean nothing is happening. It means that regardless of what arises—thoughts, bodily sensations, anything around us—the mind does not react with its entrenched habit of clinging to what we like and hating what we dislike. The entrenched habit of reifying the unfolding present moment into a fixed entity, an object of our like and dislike, is also released. There is clarity about what is happening but not habitual reactivity; hence the mind is "unmoving." It is not about being oblivious or numb.

The practice is also not about indulging in this blissful stillness. "Cleansing the mind" does not mean getting rid of unacceptable thoughts; that would be agitating the mind like pressing down ripples on the lake. The cleansing involves the nonactivation of our entrenched habit of reacting to the present moment. Instead, no matter what arises in the mind, let through, let be, let go . . . moment after moment. As the mind is less agitated and muddied by our habitual striving—directing the mind here and there—there is illumination of all as it is. With this clarity of a still mind, we can clearly see our interconnectedness and respond appropriately to do what needs to be done to benefit everyone, including ourselves, in accordance with wisdom and compassion.

HONGZHI, DAHUI, AND
SPIRITUAL BYPASSING

Master Hongzhi, mentioned in the previous section, was the founder and first great articulator and teacher of Silent Illumination who changed the course of Chinese Chan practice and whose teachings inspired the thirteenth-century Japanese Master Dōgen's lineage of Soto Zen. It is from Hongzhi's writings that our understanding of Silent Illumination originates. He taught that "in this silent sitting, whatever realms may appear, the mind is very clear as to all the details, yet everything is where it originally is, in its own place. The mind stays on one thought for ten thousand years, yet does not dwell on any forms, inside or outside."[5]

Hongzhi's great friend and Dharma colleague Master Dahui was known to be a critic of Silent Illumination, but in fact, he was a critic of the *incorrect practice* of Silent Illumination. As Simon Child points out, it is helpful to pay attention to Master Dahui's critiques to understand the pitfalls along the way because Master Dahui was speaking to experienced practitioners and warning against quietism. After we've settled the scattered and confused mind, we must not become complacent; we shouldn't cling to stillness and consider it enlightenment. People hear the word *silence* and think, "Oh, that means nothing in the mind. How do I get rid of everything?" instead of cultivating clear awareness of the subtle activities of the mind. That is not Silent Illumination. In fact, it can lead to another meditative hazard: spiritual bypassing.

Spiritual bypassing is defined as "the tendency to use spiritual ideas and practices to sidestep or avoid facing unresolved emotional issues, psychological wounds, and unfinished developmental tasks."[6] Although brought into the vernacular in the late twentieth century by the American Buddhist psychotherapist and author John Welwood, spiritual bypassing is not a modern concept. It is not a new discovery. However, it is a real and common problem that is very much not Silent Illumination.

Perpetuating a dull mind, a mind that is oblivious, or a mind that is intentionally unaware is a subtle way of hiding—a form of spiritual bypassing. We purposely do not see problematic things that are going on. It may be excusing abuse, microaggressions, a damaging way of relating to other people, or allowing ourselves to be treated poorly and deliberately cultivating a lack of awareness, an oblivious attitude to justify staying in an unhealthy situation, all the while thinking it is "good" practice. That is spiritual bypassing.

Silent Illumination is not a way to gloss over or dodge our problems or the troubles of the world. Silence and illumination are two sides of the same coin, illumination being the function of silence—when the mind does not succumb to habitual reactivity. Likewise, Silent Illumination is not passive, it is not a blank or dead mind. Remember: it is the method of no-method, not the method of no thoughts, feelings, or activities, nor the method of no discernment. It is about being willing to investigate our lives at an experiential level. As we practice, it is not that the mind is doing nothing; the mind is allowing each moment to be fully experienced as it is. We are a body and mind right here and right now, and Silent Illumination offers an opportunity to see the true nature of our existence—that we are wholly interconnected, cocreating each emerging present moment.

NOTHING TO ATTAIN

Just as Silent Illumination is neither quietism, a deadening of mind, nor a way to bypass the troubles in our heads and the world, it is not something we can achieve or attain—there is no state of Silent Illumination we can preserve in a bottle for eternity! Often, after practitioners experience very deep stillness, they believe that is what it is. And so, they hold on to this goal, thinking, "I have achieved Silent Illumination!" They try to recreate and return to that experience. This is an erroneous view because Silent Illumination is not an experience to be sought, held on to, or returned to. It is a way to be fully engaged in life, moment after moment.

In the Diamond Sutra, a record of a discourse between the Buddha and one of his senior disciples, Subhuti, the Buddha reminds us:

> It is impossible to retain past mind,
> Impossible to hold on to present mind,
> And impossible to grasp future mind.[7]

In fact, no mind can be attained because every moment is the coming together of constantly changing causes and conditions— it is unattainable. It is an experience; it goes away. You cannot freeze a moment and keep it for eternity as much as you might like to do so. If you are meditating in search of a souvenir, trophy, or accomplishment, you may want to give up the idea.

Likewise, another important Buddhist text in Chan, the Heart Sutra, teaches,

There is no ignorance
or ending of ignorance,
through to no aging and death
or ending of aging and death.
There is no suffering, no cause of suffering,
no cessation of suffering, and no path.
There is no wisdom and no attainment.[8]

There it is again: *there is no wisdom and no attainment . . .* nothing to attain. When we notice we might be striving for attainment, or if we believe we have attained something in our meditation that makes us special—better and wiser than others—that is not Silent Illumination. Recognize if you are holding this erroneous view, because it is a serious obstacle in your practice.

More common is what happens when we have a pleasant meditative experience. Perhaps your body is fully relaxed, your mind is still, and you think, "That is how I am supposed to feel in meditation. That is how I am supposed to *do* meditation. I am going to try to feel like that again." Instead of allowing yourself to be with what is happening right now in meditation and staying with that just as that, you are telling yourself, "I should be feeling differently." Recognize that this wanting to attain a state is a path toward suffering because whatever is happening right now seems to not be good enough, and you are seeking to acquire another experience. You want to return to a calmness or relaxation that no longer exists. If you give that up and allow yourself to be right here and right now, you will be in a place of true relaxation and peace.

There is no need to force ourselves to let go of these entrenched habits. Doing this is often counterproductive—we may identify with our habits even more. We must practice moment after moment and not be concerned with how much progress we have made. Just allow ourselves to be transformed by the practice, gently and gradually. The moment we remember to practice, we are free from the habit of suffering; the moment we forget, we suffer. The more we practice Silent Illumination, the more we remember, gradually unlearning the habits that cause suffering.

Some people may imagine that such transformation necessarily involves turning our life upside down, changing jobs or relationships or moving to a new home. Occasionally, adjustments in our life may be needed, yet for most of us, our life may not look very different externally. We prepare and eat our meals, look after and spend time with our loved ones, solve problems at work, interact with people we encounter throughout the day, read the news, enjoy some entertainment, engage in mundane daily activities. Whatever we do, we are fully present, clearly aware of the moment-to-moment coming together of causes and conditions manifesting as the body, mind, and world around us in this stillness. Everything exists. There may be suffering but it's not a problem. We know it's conditioned, and we can choose to stop generating more suffering. We may encounter favorable conditions or adversity. We can face each moment with clarity, discernment, gratitude, and compassion as we remember not to activate unhelpful habits of discontent, agitation, hatred, and greed. Even amid great travails of life—death, sickness, turmoil in the family and society—our mind can be at ease, content and joyful and ready to serve for the benefit of all.

3

CHAN IS LIVING A
FULLY ENGAGED LIFE
What the Buddha Taught

As you progress, you will see that recognizing what is and is not Silent Illumination will help you recognize your habits and vexations and how you have been getting in the way of living a fully engaged life by creating your own suffering. For example, if you tend to try to make your meditation a particular way because you think that is how your calm mind is supposed to be, you may be doing the same thing at home because you think that is how a happy or successful family is supposed to be. Perhaps you tell yourself, "People are supposed to be like this and do this. They never speak badly about each other; they never criticize each other. Kids never misbehave." Things like that. You have created an ideal, and you are holding on to that picture to criticize your reality.

Silent Illumination practice is more than just integrated and woven into the fabric of our lives: it *is* our lives. Understanding this will help us to understand Chan within the context of the life story and basic teachings of the Buddha.

Chan is buddha-dharma—the teaching of Buddhism taken as a whole. It is a Chinese school or lineage of East Asian Buddhism. Chan is the Mandarin Chinese pronunciation of the Chinese character that is pronounced as Zen in Japanese. Although there are considerable similarities, they are not one and the same. The Chinese word *Chan* translates to mean "meditation." It comes from the Sanskrit *dhyana*, which refers to collectedness of mind and meditative absorption. Yet around the sixth century C.E., the Chinese term had also come to describe the community of monks who specialized in meditation. Chan teachings were introduced to Japan in the seventh century but were not established as a separate Buddhist school there until the twelfth century, evolving into what we now call Zen. There is sometimes a misperception that the development of Chan ended then in China. In his scholarly works, Master Sheng Yen explains that Chan did not cease developing in China; rather, often for economic or political reasons, it changed form.[9] For example, during the Ming dynasty (1368–1644), Chan teachings were preserved in monasteries and temples that centered on Pure Land Buddhism—the most widely practiced form of Buddhism in East Asia—whereas in Japan, Zen became a separate sect. In other words, in Japan Pure Land is distinct from Zen, but in China Pure Land and Chan were often practiced within the same monasteries and temples. Chan is seen as a component of Chinese Buddhism—it is not separate, which is how Chan survived over the past five hundred years.

Master Sheng Yen (1930–2009) was one of the first Chinese monastics to teach Chan practice to Westerners in the United

States when he arrived in New York in the mid-1970s. Before him, Master Hsuan Hua started teaching Chan to Westerners in California in 1962. Similar to how Zen has been, and continues to be, taught in the United States, Master Sheng Yen also emphasized the importance of practice in daily life in addition to sitting meditation. He conducted his first seven-day intensive Chan retreat in 1977 in New York, founding the Chan Meditation Center in Queens, New York, in 1979 and later the Dharma Drum Retreat Center in Pine Bush, New York, in 1997. Eventually, his lay Dharma heirs opened centers in Europe. Chan is currently practiced throughout Asia, Europe, and North America.

Chan has evolved to suit the needs of the communities in which it takes root but remains at its core a project of liberation through the process of self-exploration. This has been possible because the practice of Chan is not limited to sitting meditation, nor does it take any specific form. Chan is daily life, and we can engage in it particularly through Silent Illumination regardless of the activity, thought, or worry of the moment. Chan takes place both on and off the meditation cushion, which is one of the reasons it is especially accessible to laypeople with a contemporary and/or primarily Western orientation.

CHAN IS ABOUT PENETRATING THE MIND

Just because Chan is accessible doesn't mean it is lax or vague. The practice is to cultivate clarity and discernment to see how our entrenched habits of reactivity cause suffering and choose not to perpetuate these unhelpful habits. When Chan practitioners practice Silent Illumination in meditation, moment after moment they are cultivating clear awareness, directly experiencing everything as it is regardless of how challenging it might be. We are not just resting, spacing out, or sitting doing nothing.

The act of sitting is important because Chan is an embodied practice. Just as with thoughts and mind, Chan is not about ridding ourselves of physical sensations but about acknowledging and fully experiencing them. Think about this: You always have your body with you. This makes it a wonderful meditation tool because, guess what? Your body can only be here in the present moment. Your body cannot be someplace else in the future, and it cannot return to the past. You are here. Body and mind are intimately connected. This is why it is precious to have the body to practice with, so make use of it. Be grateful your mind can always follow your body back to the present moment.

Master Sheng Yen commented on this aspect of Chan, saying, "The things we teach are many: sitting postures, movements, ways of walking and prostrating, guides to contemplation and energy. These are all for tempering and harmonizing the body as well as retrieving a mind lost in illusion."[10] Chan meditation is not about creating nothingness. Master Sheng Yen used to talk about it like this: if you sit there and ignore your mind and your body, it is like soaking a stone in cold water. What do you think is going to happen?

Nothing.

You are not practicing. You might be physically and mentally still, but you are just resting, maybe vegging out or even blissing out. You can sit there all day like that if you choose, but be clear that it is not what Chan practice is. Chan practice is cultivating clarity so that we can see plainly how we get in the way of ourselves, how we generate and perpetuate suffering, and how releasing these unhelpful habits is wisdom and compassion.

John Crook addressed this misunderstanding by often repeating an important truth: Chan is not supposed to be comfortable. Why? Because if you are really doing the work, if you are genuinely cultivating clear awareness, you will be confronting yourself when you look at your modes of operation—the aspects of your habits and your life that you have been using to avoid the present moment. Maybe that is why you took up meditation in the first place. You thought you could relax and not have to notice or deal with your stuff; you could be free. Remember, the purpose of Chan (or pretty much any Buddhist practice) is to free ourselves from the habit of suffering. However, the ways most of us go about it—the usual modes of operation that we'll explore in this book—are not the ways to do it. We often put additional obstacles on the path toward reconnecting with our true self and disguise them as signs that we are good, serious, devoted meditators. These modes of operation generate suffering and will likely lead to the opposite of what you seek—the more you meditate this way, the more will you suffer.

The thing is, the habit of suffering was there all along, but when you practice Silent Illumination, you become more aware of *how* you suffer, of how you generate your own suffering. Students have complained to me saying, "Chan practice screwed up my life. I was fine before . . . perfectly fine. Meditation is the cause of my suffering." Really? Reflect on how you have been suffering all along in one way or another on and off the cushion. You just haven't been aware of it. Chan is an opportunity for you to notice and acknowledge your suffering, so that you can stop giving rise to more of it—let through, let be, let go—which is why it is ultimately *a project of liberation through the process of self-exploration.*

When we talk about liberation or freedom from suffering, many people like to think it is an unreachable state, something holy, but it is grounded in the right here and right now. Ask yourself, "What is going on with me?" Do you know what is happening in the unfolding present moment? What is the obstacle between you and your liberation? Silent Illumination can allow you to answer clearly, honestly, because chances are those same habits, the same ways of generating suffering in your meditation, operate in your daily life. You may be able to make those connections as soon as you allow yourself to acknowledge them. You might come to say, "I am so critical of myself when I meditate, but that is how I treat other people. I am so harsh and impatient with everyone. Wow . . ."

Now you see why John Crook said, "Chan is not supposed to be comfortable." It can be quite disconcerting, difficult, or shocking to see your modes of operation and confront yourself, but that is the work. As you meditate, you may fantasize about a perfect life or you may think, "Okay, I'll worry about it later" or "I need to do this now and work hard so that I can get enlightened and then everything will be fine." There is a belief that if you meditate the "right" way all your problems will be gone. That is not ending your suffering, and it is certainly not enlightenment; you are wishing for something other than what is and seeking relief or escape from the present moment. That is not staying with things just as they are.

Everyone encounters difficulties—Master Sheng Yen had them, the Buddha had them, I do, and so do you—that is part of living on earth. Chan practice is not about troubleshooting, asceticism, or making our mind "pure" or into any particular state. It is about seeing into the true nature of reality by understanding how our mind actually works, and, just as the Buddha did, you can begin doing that right now.

THE BUDDHA, EMBODIMENT, AND THE MODES OF OPERATION

When we talk about the Buddha, we are not talking about a god or a deity. We are talking about our original teacher of the Dharma, Shakyamuni Buddha, who was a human being, a son, a father, and who lived on earth about twenty-five hundred years ago. He went through a lot of difficulties to discover what ultimately became Buddhist practice, to reveal a way out of our unsatisfactory human condition, a way out of our sense of lacking. And he realized that we do not have to experience life that way. There is a different way of being. Not only that, but he also committed his life to skillfully sharing what he discovered and finding ways to explain the practice and his teachings for people with different causes and conditions, different levels of spiritual development, and even different vexations and modes of operation. No matter whom he was with—be they kings, beggars, or disciples—he was consistently able to treat that person with compassion and wisdom. No small feat if we have ever tried this ourselves.

It is helpful to understand how Shakyamuni Buddha got to this point. If you are not familiar with the Buddha's story, there is value in hearing what it has to tell us because he went through life—experiencing joy and suffering—just like we all do. He taught that precisely because he was a human being like us and this was something he could do, we all could do it too if we engaged in the practice. He was not superhuman.

The Buddha's story started with his noticing the experiences of suffering. He was born into an aristocratic family in what we now call Nepal and lived in comfort, but as a young man, when he left his palace for the first time and saw sick, old, and dead people, something shifted within him. We might have had a similar experience when we were relatively young. Usually, people first realize the fragility of life when someone they know or a pet passes away or becomes gravely ill, but before that, we feel like we can live forever; we are completely oblivious. We believe, "That is someone else's business" because it is an abstract thing that we have not yet experienced. We tend not to think of sickness and death as an integral part of our human condition like we do with birth, love, and satisfaction.

When we encounter someone's death, it is a shock to everyone, and in that moment we might be struck hard by the realization, "Wow, we are mortal!" Then, after the astonishment wears off, it may become, "I'll count my blessings and then try to move on and not think about it very much." Shakyamuni Buddha's response was neither avoidance nor intellectualization. He basically said, "Yeah, suffering is our condition." He took it very seriously, but he didn't let it depress or paralyze him. Instead, he tried to figure out what to do. He asked, "Is there a way out of this?"

What he first realized was that how he had been living life was not the way out of suffering. He had no shortage of luxury, meaning he could engage in whatever sensory pleasures he wished. He had plentiful food, beautiful clothes, a majestic home, lovely wives—whatever he wanted. Think about this in the context of your own life. How much of it have you spent striving for money, status, comfort, and the nicest clothes, home, second home, vacation, or whatever has been on your bucket list, only to attain them and still feel like it is not enough?

I have encountered many such people who have said things to me like "Yep, I am forty years old. I have achieved everything I wish to achieve in life. I am successful and have plenty of money, but I do not feel happy. I do not feel fulfilled at all." So, they came to meditation practice like Shakyamuni Buddha, realizing that indulging in sensory pleasures, whatever they might be, is not the way. It is important to remember the Buddha had all of that and the resources to get even more if he wanted to, but he realized it wasn't going to end suffering.

I am not advocating you quit your job or leave your family and home, but remember that you can have a job, a home, and the stuff that you own and still realize these in themselves are not going to help free you from suffering. Many people would disagree with me. For them it is "If I get this next promotion, I'll be happy"; "If I can get married and have my two babies, I am going to be complete"; "If I make enough money to buy my dream car, I am going to be content." Many people spend their whole lives like this, suffering in a place of "if" and far, far from awakening.

The Buddha left his life of nice stuff behind. He set out on a spiritual journey becoming an ascetic (or beggar, depending on the version of the story). He joined many religious practitioners engaging in all kinds of yogic rituals and meditative practices. When he began to meditate, he was able to enter a deep *samadhi* state right away. In the Buddha's time, before

Buddhism, samadhi—a union with the Divine in deep meditative absorption—was regarded as the ultimate stage of meditation. His samadhi states were intense and blissful. In fact, that is what some people chase after or want to acquire when they engage in meditation, yet as you will see, it is ultimately a mode of operation. The Buddha mastered the method to enter these blissful states and found they were far more sublime than the ordinary sensory pleasures we experience from eating fine food, wearing beautiful clothing, and having power or adoration. But unlike some people who become addicted to these samadhi states, he realized that this was not *it*—this was not the way out of suffering. When he was meditating and in an absorbed, blissful state, it was marvelous; however, the moment he emerged, nothing had changed—there was still sickness, old age, death, war, hatred, unsatisfactoriness, and suffering of all sorts.

Bliss, trance, and meditative absorption are not the ultimate destination or answer. Some people do not believe this. Some of us practice and practice and become very good meditators, experts at getting into deep states of meditative absorption. How do we go about it? Simply by spending more and more time meditating. Throughout history people have left home, gone into the mountains, monasteries, and caves, and dedicated themselves to meditation. You could do it if you really wanted to—just abandon your responsibilities and spend all your time meditating. But remember, as soon as you are out of that meditative state, you still suffer. The habitual tendencies that cause suffering are still activated when interacting with others. You haven't really done much to liberate yourself, or anyone else for that matter. You are just hiding in these meditative absorptions.

The Buddha saw that no matter how seductive, no matter how enjoyable, meditative absorption wasn't the answer, so he decided to engage in ascetic practices. Asceticism was a common form of spiritual training in ancient India and still is among some Hindu sects (though it is not exclusive to India; for example, you might have heard stories of Christian penitents whipping or torturing themselves, inflicting pain to overcome their corporeal bodies). It is about seeing our body as the source of suffering. The body experiences desire, needs to be fed, and wants to be comfortable, so asceticism is about depriving the physical self of all that—figuratively or even literally beating desire out of the body, starving it of what it craves.

The Buddha became serious about this. You might have read about the ascetics of his day who did all kinds of intense stuff, like not sleeping indoors and definitely not sleeping on a mattress—which makes it pretty difficult to have a comfortable night's sleep—or fasting to the point of starvation. But how is this different from inflicting emotional pain as a way to transcend ourselves? Reflect on whether you engage in a certain kind of asceticism without intending to—depriving yourself of what you reasonably need—and believe you are practicing well by so doing.

When the Buddha engaged in asceticism he grew very weak—he saw that in his effort to end suffering he'd indulged a new way to suffer. He realized, "Maybe I've been doing something wrong. Maybe I've been going about it incorrectly." Not because he couldn't hack it anymore but because he didn't see it as being a way out of suffering. So, to the horror of his fellow ascetics, when a young woman offered him a cup of rice and milk, he accepted just enough food to sustain his body.

This is very important. There is a reason why this is part of his story. It is a moment when Shakyamuni Buddha accepted that he was a human being, that he had a body. Having a body that needs to be fed is part of being human. Having a body that needs rest is part of being human. All our effort, all our striving to transcend having this human body takes us nowhere and clearly doesn't end suffering. Yet, as human beings we keep looking for different ways to try to transcend this reality of having a body.

We wage a war against reality our entire life. Here we are, born with this body that needs to be fed, that needs some basic care. We get it into our head that something's wrong. Pain, disease, illness—it is part of having nerve cells that send signals to your brain, and the brain is part of your functioning body. Imagine the alternative: no body, or a body that has no sensation, no neurons, no brain, or a brain that doesn't work. That we can experience anything is a miracle. Think about that when you get disgusted with your body. This is actually an important part of the practice of Silent Illumination, and we need to take it seriously and integrate it into our practice.

Our unwillingness to accept this reality is quite pervasive. Of course, it comes with resisting the fact that this body is not permanent. It gets sick. It ages. It doesn't stay one way. It is not fully in our control. As time passes, it doesn't look the same, like it did ten years ago. Your hair won't stay the same color, maybe won't even stay on your head. The face changes, the skin changes. We endure an incredible amount of suffering in our refusal to accept the reality of our body. Our society offers all kinds of remedies—like anti-wrinkle cream, diets, and hair-growing unguents—to reverse aging. Use them all if you like, but bear in mind that it is the refusal to accept the reality of having this body, not the aging itself, that causes the suffering.

After the Buddha accepted the rice and milk, what did he do next? He sat down under a fig tree—the Bodhi tree. He just sat; *he stayed with that, just as that.* It is important to pay attention here. *He just sat down.* He didn't sit down to fight his thoughts, or change them, make them better, or suppress them; he didn't sit down to induce extraordinary states of mind. He just sat there. He sat in total clear awareness of everything that was going on in his body and mind, everything . . . *everything* without exception.

If you are familiar with the Buddha's story, you might remember that part of his meditation under the Bodhi tree included the demon-king Mara who tempted the Buddha with beautiful women and sexual seduction. I do not know how you interpreted that story, but many understand it as "Buddha was really good at resisting temptation." That is not quite it. The real story was that he allowed the temptation to show up in his mind. He could have thought, "Ooh, I like naked women, but I shouldn't be thinking about that. Ooh . . . I like sex, but I shouldn't be thinking about that." He could have rejected, fought, suppressed, denied, or tried to change the situation or pretended that what was there wasn't, not allowing it to be as it is. He didn't do this. He let Mara introduce the powerful seduction into his mind. The Buddha sat there and allowed it to come through like a movie but did not become entangled in or overtaken by it. He didn't resist; he didn't leave. He saw the true nature of everything that went through his mind as impermanent and empty of independent self-nature. These powerful images and feelings arose and perished. He didn't need to do anything.

After a week of meditation under the Bodhi tree, he looked up into the sky and saw the morning star. Some people interpret this as a reason to go to India, to find that tree, meditate, look up, and think, "Where's the star? Is that what I am going to get enlightened by?" But that is not the point. What is? "Every tree as it is. Every star as it is. Everything as it is. Not a problem." This is the opposite of "Whatever is in the present moment is not good enough. Whatever is going on right now is not how it is supposed to be. The star is not bright enough. I wish there were more stars . . ." That is how we usually experience ourselves in the world, but when the Buddha awakened, he realized, "Everything is still here. There is no problem. No problem whatsoever." *Total acceptance*. Acceptance here does not mean it is how it is supposed to be or that we deserve it. Total acceptance arises with the realization that every moment is the unique coming together of all the causes and conditions in the entire universe. Everything is perfect as it is. Not a single thing is missing. There is no idea of anything needing to be changed or added. It is just thus.

Often this state is referred to as the extinction of suffering. There is no craving, no feeling of "I want more" or "This part needs to be changed or erased." Nothing. Whatever is here is perfect as it is. There is peace, but this peace is different from what you imagine when you try to create it. The peace I am talking about is silence, the silence in Silent Illumination.

As you can see, during Shakyamuni Buddha's meditation, a lot went on; very powerful things moved through his mind along with huge temptations and criticism from the external world, but that was not a problem because he didn't try to change, deny, suppress, or block any of it. He didn't say, "This thought is not what I want. This action is not supposed to be here. I want something different . . . something better. I want something more sublime . . . more spiritual." That is not silence; it is reacting, labeling, judging, comparing it against something you have created in your mind about how it is supposed to be and how the present moment is falling short. It is strategizing about how you can make it better, change it, get rid of it.

Whatever comes through the mind is not a problem, and with it comes illumination. In the Buddha's story this is illustrated by the utter, total clear awareness—he knew exactly what it was. Like the Buddha, we can experience life fully as it is. No matter what thoughts or feelings appear, everything is Silent Illumination.

We can learn from the Buddha's example of being willing to overcome difficulties; we can learn from his wisdom, his compassion, his practice, his commitment, and his *illuminating silence*. There is a way of being that is different from the way we have been living, and as the Buddha showed us, it is one of clarity, awakening, and loving-kindness that he explained for us in the Four Noble Truths.

4

A WAY OF SEEING
The Four Noble Truths

When Shakyamuni Buddha emerged from his enlightenment to share what he realized through direct experience, he articulated his teachings in what is known as the Four Noble Truths. In the first noble truth, he pointed out that there is suffering (*dukkha*) that needs to be fully acknowledged, not denied. Then he explained the cause of suffering as the entrenched habit of reacting to whatever is happening with vexations (kleshas) in the second truth. When we react to what is going on with vexation, we suffer. We are then prone to react to our suffering by giving rise to more vexations, resulting in more suffering. This vicious cycle of suffering is *samsara*. The good news is that he discovered—as articulated in the third truth—that suffering is not inevitable; because suffering is conditioned by its cause, we can choose to not give rise to the cause of suffering. Nirvana is the cessation of the cycle of suffering. In the fourth truth, he detailed the cultivation of the Eightfold Path, which is encompassed in the practice of Silent Illumination, as the prescription for freeing us from the unhelpful habits of generating suffering for ourselves and others.

In other words, the Buddha discovered that life may be difficult and challenging at times, but by training the mind it is possible not to succumb to the entrenched habits of the mind that generate suffering. We can fully embrace life by staying with this just as this—moment after moment—in the practice of Silent Illumination. Whatever is happening, however difficult or amazing, since it already happened, we allow it to be here, fully experienced, felt, and seen, and allow it to move on as life continues to unfold. We clearly see that each emerging present moment is the coming together of causes and conditions, recognizing what a wondrous miracle every instant of life is, even when things are challenging. We can be fully at ease even amid great turmoil or temptation.

The Buddha is often described as a physician whose teachings in the Four Noble Truths can be understood as the diagnosis and cure for the disease of suffering. This is a helpful way to understand the Buddha's teachings so as not to mistake the Four Noble Truths for abstract principles or absolutes we must blindly believe. Doing so will not get us very far. When we see the teachings of the Four Noble Truths as a diagnosis, we understand the importance of cultivating clear awareness of our direct experience of suffering. If we do not know that we are sick, we will not see the need to take the medicine. If we do not recognize that we, like everyone else, suffer, we will not see the need to practice. When we first get started on the path, we forget to practice because we are not convinced that we really need to. The more we practice, the more we realize that we need to practice. After a while, we cannot imagine not practicing. Practice is life.

However, we must be careful not to take the analogy of suffering as disease too far. Watch your tendency to think of being sick as bad or not how we are supposed to be and developing a resultant aversion to suffering by turning it into a fixed entity to get rid of in meditation practice. That would be a grave mistake. We perpetuate the habits that generate suffering if we practice this way. The key point of the Buddha's teachings in the Four Noble Truths is that suffering is the coming together of causes and conditions—our experience living as a human being and habit of reacting with vexations. Sickness, aging, and death are natural. The emotions we experience in challenging and wonderful situations are also natural. They do not constitute suffering by themselves. It is when these experiences of being human come together with vexations that suffering results. It's like adding heat to water and steam results. We are so habituated to reacting with vexations that suffering is our familiar way of being. That's why the Buddha pointed this fact out in the first noble truth. He did not say, "You are a failure, and something is wrong with you if you suffer." It's more like "Let's face it, we all suffer, and guess what? There is a different way to be in which we don't suffer and cause harm to others." This does not involve going anywhere else. All we need to do is to be fully here, staying with this just as this in Silent Illumination.

Suffering is a word that gets used a lot in discussions of Buddhism, but what exactly is it? Let's return to our simple formula: the experience of the present moment + vexation = suffering. You can apply this formula to any aspect of life:

Reading about politics in the newspaper + hating
   politicians = suffering
Children throwing a tantrum + wishing they'd have more
   self-control = suffering
Seeing another person enjoying their life + wishing your
   life was like theirs = suffering
Thoughts arising in sitting meditation + getting
   frustrated = suffering
Enjoying a beautiful day with blue sky + wanting more
   days like this = suffering

Suffering is an agitated mind. When we suffer, we are disconnected from Silent Illumination. Rather than experiencing reality as it is, it is an entrenched habit of feeling that whatever is right here, right now is not good enough, not how it is supposed to be: "I am not calm enough. Our relationship is not close enough. I wish that person could be different—more thoughtful, more open-minded, more caring, more successful . . . I hate being in this situation." That mind of unsatisfactoriness is insidious and ubiquitous, which brings us to the first noble truth.

THE FIRST NOBLE TRUTH

The first noble truth teaches that suffering is a fact of typical human existence.

When you meditate, do you experience leg pain or perhaps drowsiness? Maybe you sit, struggling to make your mind calm while thinking, "I do not want this mind and I do not want that mind . . . I want another one." Not only is that the opposite of Silent Illumination—of staying with that just as that, staying with this just as this—it is an embodiment of the first noble truth: *There is suffering.* Even the privilege of having the time, space, and knowledge to meditate can be turned into suffering.

Our inclination to resist reality is a reason why the Buddha started with suffering because the initial order of business is to fully recognize how much we suffer in many different ways. Perhaps somewhere inside you have been feeling that something is missing in your life. You do not quite know what is missing, but you know you want to find it. There is a sense of lack, or maybe you feel a nagging belief that something is wrong or simply not quite right or not quite right enough. Maybe that is why you decided to try meditation in the first place—to find out what that "something" is. Or perhaps to find out how you can fix yourself?

In his very first sermon about the Four Noble Truths, the Buddha spoke about dukkha, which is usually translated as "suffering," although I prefer the term *unsatisfactoriness* or *feeling unsatisfactory*. This suffering or unsatisfactoriness refers to our experiencing whatever is in the present moment as not being good enough. Right here, right now, as you are reading this book, whatever you are feeling, whatever you are experiencing, is it satisfactory? Do you wish to be more comfortable, less tired, more motivated, less distracted? Whatever it is, is there something that is not enough? Is there something about this moment in time that is not how it is "supposed" to be?

How do you even know exactly how this unfolding brand-new present moment is supposed to be? You have never been in this moment. Where exactly did you get your criteria? From the past? But the past was a different moment, and each moment is the coming together of fresh causes and conditions. It is a curious way to go about our life if you think about it, believing we already know how this moment is supposed to be when we can't possibly know exactly how this moment will unfold. Yet, it is a common response.

Taking this a step further: do we even know that we experience this unsatisfactoriness, this suffering? Chances are in your daily life, you may have only a vague sense of it because, after all, you are really busy. But what came first? Perhaps we allow our lives to become so busy and complicated, filled with appointments, tasks, to-do lists, and commitments, that we never have a moment to face this unsatisfactoriness.

I've found when people stop and look at themselves this way, they do not like what they see . . . at least at first. They notice that their mind is more out of control than they thought. Without understanding that is how an untrained mind tends to be, they think something is wrong with them. Some people even complain, "I was fine *before* I meditated. Now I am angry and resentful." Did they turn bitter as a result of meditating? Probably not. More likely, what happened was they were suffering without being aware of it. When they started to meditate and allowed the mind to settle, they became aware of their suffering. This is actually good news. They realized what the Buddha was talking about: there is suffering. When we do not allow ourselves a moment to reflect, to be here, we might not notice how much suffering we are experiencing, how this feeling of unsatisfactoriness arises moment after moment after moment. If we can just keep our mind occupied with our phone or TV, reading, gossiping, or any activity, we can keep ourselves from noticing unsatisfactoriness—we can pretend we are not suffering. Perhaps this is why we have the culture we have. There is no shortage of stuff to keep us from noticing this aspect of our existence—unsatisfactoriness.

Some people say Buddhism is a downer. "We talk so much about suffering. Why can't we just talk about something more pleasant? More uplifting?" Comments like this reflect a misunderstanding of what suffering means. What I have been focusing on is called pervasive suffering—the nagging sense that something is not quite right even though there is nothing obviously amiss. That's what I experienced when I first started practicing. My family was fine, my work was going well, and I was young and healthy. Hence the translation "unsatisfactoriness" for *dukkha* here would resonate more easily when talking about pervasive suffering.

We encounter extremely difficult and painful things as human beings. Our body gets sick, deteriorates as it ages, and goes through the dying process. It's difficult to watch our loved ones going through these painful experiences. We don't always get what we strive for. We experience the pain of being separated from our loved ones and of living in challenging situations. Living with a body and in relationships can be quite difficult at times. We make it more difficult and experience what is called suffering of suffering (*dukkha dukkha*) when we react to the reality of living with a body with vexations such as hating being sick or getting older. When vexation does not arise, we can be at peace amid the pain brought by sickness, aging, and death and see clearly that all is causes and conditions. With vexations, people can suffer a great deal and inflict a lot of pain on others as they get older even without serious illness.

Of course, life is not all about sickness, aging, death, failure, and separation. We may find ourselves enjoying our life, loving our job and our family and our community. It's easy to fall into the belief that this is how things are supposed to be and to forget impermanence. When things change, we suffer. Hence, when the Buddha pointed out that there is suffering, it does not necessarily mean we are in agony all the time. We can be enjoying a family reunion and give rise to suffering when we crave for the happy time to last forever. This is called suffering of change (*viparinama dukkha*). By stating, "There is suffering" as the first noble truth, the Buddha was helping us see that we suffer and encouraging us to pay attention to our suffering.

Why does this matter? Why should we pay attention? When we don't know we suffer and are not aware of our mind being agitated, we are more likely to cause harm to ourselves and others. When we are aware that we are suffering, we know our mind is agitated and that the lack of clarity distorts our perception of the situation. Recognizing this helps us be more discerning, reflecting more carefully on the motivation of our action. Before we speak or act, we ask, "Am I doing this as revenge because I blame my suffering on this person? Or am I doing this to contribute to the resolution of the situation?" We may notice that there are traces of the former and it is unwise to proceed.

Without clear awareness of our subtle thoughts and feelings, our true motivation may be obscured by clever rationalization of our actions, convincing ourselves we are doing something good when it is actually the perpetuation of our habit of aversion. Without clear awareness of how we suffer, we are prone to succumb to the entrenched habit of reacting to what is unpleasant with aversion without even knowing that we are doing so. When we are not aware of our hating the fact that a happy family reunion is about to end and we have to part with our loved ones, our mind is so clouded with suffering that we may mistakenly believe it is the family gathering that is causing our suffering and start lashing out at everyone, ruining the gathering for them as well as ourselves. With clear awareness of our habit of craving more of this happy time with the family, vexation does not take over as easily. Remembering that every moment is the coming together of causes and conditions, gratitude for this precious moment allows us to fully experience the entirety of the reunion, causing less suffering for self and others.

When we are not at peace, everything we see is a problem because we are experiencing the world through the lens of an agitated mind. Someone may do something kind for us, and we feel they are bothering us. We can't see the action and feel the gratitude that naturally arises when we open our hearts to this kindness. Or we might overfocus on someone's choice in life and nitpick, criticize, and want to fix them. When we suffer and do not realize it, we are prone to taking it out on others and truly believe that they deserve our judgment, harsh words, and aggressive actions. You've likely encountered someone who is upset, talking louder and louder, and when someone said, "Do not be so angry," they replied yelling, "I am not angry! I am calm. You are making me angry!" They have no idea how angry they are, no idea that their mind is agitated, distorting their perception. When there is no clarity in the mind, one is prone to misjudgment, making it difficult to respond to the situation appropriately. That is why the initial teaching, the first noble truth, is to become aware that we are suffering.

When we are engaged in the practice of Silent Illumination,

we begin to notice how we suffer and how we cause our suffering. It might be something minor, like being upset because we're not getting the food we want for dinner or because our chair is uncomfortable. Or it might be something more serious, like "I hate all the changes at work" or "I wish my dad would stop getting depressed." It's all suffering.

Notice this agitation in your mind. Perhaps you will say, "I know who caused my suffering. It is the restaurant that prepared such a lousy dinner" or "It's my partner who forgets to fix the chair no matter how many times I ask." Perhaps you believe, "It is my boss who made my life miserable at work" or "It's my dad's depression." No matter the situation you think, "If things were the way I wanted them, I wouldn't suffer." Or maybe your coworker, your neighbor, your child is what you see as the cause of your suffering. "If I can just make them change, everything will be perfect." Haven't we all entertained these thoughts? When we believe that other people are the cause of our suffering, we give rise to hatred and believe the solution to our suffering has to do with them not us. Imagine the hatred and violence we breed in our minds. If we perpetuate this habit, should we be surprised by the violence and atrocity that human beings are capable of?

THE RIPPLE EFFECTS OF SUFFERING

Of course, it is not just about us! When we suffer, we cause suffering for others. Think about things like bullying—someone who has been bullied often goes on to harm another victim, a parent who snaps at a child for no reason plants seeds of anxiety or doubt, neglecting our environment causes suffering for generations to come. Understanding this conceptually is but the beginning. We need to experience the ways in which our suffering compels us to hurt others even though intellectually we do not want to cause harm to others.

A catalyst of suffering writ large in our culture is racism. When we suffer and want to find someone to blame, those marginalized and discriminated against in our society become ready targets. Think about it: racism is essentially dehumanizing someone, reducing another human being to an entity defined by their skin color, rather than recognizing their full humanity. When we can only see our preconceived notions of someone as conditioned by our culture and upbringing, allowing these ideas to block our awareness of the present moment, we can no longer see someone as a human with a story to which we can relate with an open heart. We have reduced this living, breathing human being to an object or a category, and this can lead us to not think twice about diminishing, dismissing, or even demonizing or harming that person. When we are not aware of such tendencies in our mind, we respond in ways that cause suffering for other people as well as ourselves. The experience of not being seen and feeling invisible, not to mention any unfair treatment they may receive, is painful and contributes to their feeling undeserving of love and respect. Hence, every time we treat someone as a category instead of seeing them for who they are, we are causing great suffering.

Sadly, we also cause suffering for ourselves because we are often unaware of how we are dehumanized in the process of our dehumanization of others. Because racial categories are defined relatively (Black versus white, white versus nonwhite, etc.), when we only see someone as white or Black or Asian and therefore as different, we can only see ourselves as not white/Black/Asian. In that moment, we lose touch with the rest of ourselves. Consequently, when we see and relate to others only as a racial category, we reduce ourselves to a category as well and cease to see ourselves as full human beings, denying ourselves the full range of our experience.

When we become aware of how the social structure of racial hierarchy is superimposed over our thinking, we begin to realize how our ways of being and relating to others have been conditioned by this structure. Through the practice of Silent Illumination we can discover that we need not choose to see people through the lens of categories. The habit is so entrenched that it may feel like we have no choice, but we do! Each moment, even though they are familiar and provide the illusion of comfort, we can choose not to repeat our vexatious habits that cause suffering for self and others. We can choose to see all as fellow humans like ourselves, free from such categories.

I am not talking about ignoring the difference in our experiences, backgrounds, worldviews, and beliefs, or the fact that this person may not even like me or that I am in love with that person. We can be keenly aware of all these differences but still choose to listen to and feel for others as fellow beings trying to cope in this world of suffering *just as we are*. When we do, even though we may disagree, we connect with ourselves and others more fully and are better able to empathize and break the pattern of suffering.

Be it embedded racism, the vicissitudes of human relationships, or something as mundane as being cut off in traffic, we do not *have* to suffer. That is what the Buddha discovered. Understanding the Four Noble Truths and applying the teachings through the practice of Silent Illumination is an effective way to disrupt the cycle of suffering, even (or perhaps especially) in our modern lives, and this is the lesson of the second noble truth.

THE SECOND NOBLE TRUTH

The second noble truth teaches that suffering is caused by the coming together of the present moment and our habitual reactivities.

You may be wondering, "What does all this talk of suffering have to do with sitting meditation? How is it going to help me?" Cultivating clarity is why we meditate. It is not for us to become champion meditators. It is for us to see into the various subtle-yet-entrenched habits of the mind—the habits of creating suffering that we do not even know. That is why the Four Noble Truths are pointers toward how we suffer and how we generate suffering for ourselves and others. Through the practice, we realize that our assumption that our suffering is caused by other people's actions is an erroneous view. I have been saying that suffering = the present moment + vexation. Upon hearing this, some people may mistakenly conclude, "I am the cause of suffering. I am the problem!" and succumb to the habit of self-hatred. That would be unfortunate.

Understanding the second noble truth is helpful here. Every moment is the coming together of causes and conditions. When we talk about how suffering comes about, for the purpose of practice, the causes and conditions that come together are conceptually divided into two categories:

- What is happening in the present moment
- Vexations

What is happening in the present moment is the coming together of causes and conditions, influenced by all that happened before. This moment is not a random accident even though it may appear so at times because we can't see the innumerable connections. If we imagine that every moment is the interaction of countless instances of the "butterfly effect," we can begin to appreciate how every moment is a miracle, and we are truly interconnected. If we try to trace every element that makes the present moment possible, we can see that everything that has ever happened will be included and the actual tracing will exceed our cognitive capacity. That's why the word *inconceivable* is often used in the sutras to describe this fact about the nature of our existence. Likewise, emptiness is one of the common translations of the word *shunyata* to convey the true nature of our being, that every moment is the coming together of causes and conditions. It does not mean that things do not exist. In fact, everything exists . . . *temporarily*. Everything we experience is the coming together of causes and conditions that are themselves the coming together of causes and conditions. Nothing, however, exists as an inherent independent entity.

We go through life believing otherwise. When we buy a ticket to see a concert, purchasing the ticket is but one of the many causes and conditions for our experience of seeing the performance. The performance is not an inherently existing entity. The training of and the support received by all the musicians and people working on and off stage were part of the causes and conditions. We can arrive at the venue on time only because our health, the weather, and road conditions, among other things, make it possible, and each is conditioned by numerous factors. The same applies to the performers. That we sit in a concert hall to enjoy music is a miracle. Yet, we tend to believe that our purchasing the ticket is all that made attending the performance possible, ignoring all the causes and conditions that need to come together. Our purchasing the ticket is one of the causes. So are the people who nurture our interest in music and our receptiveness to their actions. Those past actions cause us to show up at the performance. But while our past thoughts and actions play an important role in shaping this moment, they are not the only factors. If instead of enjoying the concert performance we are busy nitpicking how it is not as good as a past performance we have attended, we are reacting with the vexation of fundamental ignorance.

Not recognizing the true nature of reality as emptiness is the root of vexation, and this is called *avidya*, often translated as "fundamental ignorance." The Chinese characters for this term literally mean "no clarity," referring to the lack of clarity about the true nature of reality—emptiness. We lack clear awareness of our entrenched habit to take all the causes and conditions that make this moment possible for granted. We forget that each moment is brand-new; this is a different concert even if we have seen these musicians perform before. We may have little influence on how the present moment will come together, yet still we can decide whether it is a moment of suffering or not. When we fall into the habit of reifying what is happening in the present moment, forgetting it is a flow of causes and conditions, we then give rise to the feeling of like or dislike toward the entity we have created in our mind often based on our past conditioning. We crave more of what we like and hate what we dislike. Craving and aversion constitute the second and third vexations, and together with fundamental ignorance they are often called the "three poisons" of the mind by Buddhists. The habitual tendencies of reacting with fundamental ignorance, craving, and aversion are entrenched and take myriad forms. They will be discussed in detail in later chapters as various modes of operation.

The second noble truth is articulated to highlight the fact that suffering is conditioned by the convergence of what is happening in the present moment and our entrenched habit of reacting with vexations. It is not to make suffering and vexations our enemy; it is to point out that all is the coming together of causes and conditions, and we can choose not to contribute to the conditions for suffering. Each moment we remember to do so, we are free from suffering in that moment.

When causes and conditions come together for the body to fall ill, for instance, we can be fully present with each moment of pains and aches and do what needs to be done, or we can hate the fact that we are sick, blame others, and suffer. It's our choice. It is not enough to just know that we have certain habitual tendencies. These entrenched habits of mind show up quite quickly and readily because they are well-established neural pathways. They are our default modes of operation. Therefore these habits tend to show up and take over very easily even though we are conceptually aware of them. Each instance of habitual reactivity is made up of a chain of subtle thoughts and feelings—many, such as our worldview, are so pervasive that they may seem invisible early on in the practice. The practice of Silent Illumination allows us to begin to see and understand these processes. That's why cultivating moment-to-moment clear awareness is so crucial. We need to get to know our habits intimately, beyond the conceptual level, which involves practicing not just when in formal sitting meditation but when we are eating, walking, moving, working, playing, chatting, or parenting. Stay with all of that, just as all of that! Those are also the times when we will have an opportunity to see how we react to what happens in each moment of our daily lives and become familiar with our habitual reactivities at the experiential level.

You will notice that even when we are simply sitting there meditating, allowing the body to breathe, a lot can occur because of how we are reacting. Paying attention to the moment-to-moment experience of the body and mind sitting in this space helps us gain insight into our entrenched habits of reactivity that contribute to our suffering. Think about it: even when we are just sitting still, we can experience a lot of suffering. Why is that? Who is causing you to feel this? Who else but yourself! Your boss is not here. Your partner is not here. Your kids are not here. It is just you. Notice the habit of moving from blaming everyone to blaming and hating yourself. The practice is not about self-disparagement; that only blocks our entrenched habitual reactivities—aversion in this case—from our awareness and will not free us from suffering.

Meditation becomes an opportunity to see how our compulsive reactivities and our insidiously entrenched habits and beliefs show up—how we cause our own suffering. It is not just about acknowledging, "I know I am very judgmental," but seeing how our habits unfold moment after moment. As we recognize this, we can notice how our habitual reactivities are triggered and how they initiate a chain of thoughts and feelings and subtle shifts in the mind. Usually with the mind scattered, confused, and unclear, this chain of events is completely obscured. We merely find ourselves being frustrated and upset for not getting what we want, which in turn further agitates the mind, compelling us to perpetuate our habitual reactivities. When we settle the mind using our meditative practice and cultivate moment-to-moment clear awareness, we can see this chain more clearly and notice the pattern. With clarity, we can see moment after moment how we objectify and label what is going on and then identify with it by attaching certain meanings: "This is good. I like it. This is how it is supposed to be ALL the time." And inevitably, things change when causes and conditions change, and we hate it. We are stuck in constant battle with reality, resisting what is instead of staying with this just as this, in Silent Illumination. This is how we generate suffering for ourselves regardless of our circumstances, and what the second noble truth is about.

As we contemplate the second noble truth and cultivate clear awareness moment to moment, we can see more clearly when we have fallen into our entrenched habits of reacting with vexations instead of allowing this unfolding present moment to be as it is. As we see for ourselves how these unhelpful habits, our modes of operation, get in the way of our experiencing reality as it is and cause suffering for ourselves and others, we can commit to stopping perpetuating these habits.

And then what? As we learn to see these habits and become familiar with them, we grow aware of the patterns of our mind. This offers an opportunity to unlearn habitual reactivities by not perpetuating them. I like to think about it like eating potato chips. Have you ever been in a situation where you open a bag of chips, take one out and eat it, and then without knowing how it happened, you find yourself holding an empty bag? You didn't mean to eat the whole bag of chips. You told yourself,

"It just happened!" When you cultivate the practice of clear awareness, you know the chips didn't disappear on their own. You are aware of every chip as you eat it and of each time you put your hand inside the bag and take out another chip, and another . . . moment after moment. You taste each chip you put into your mouth. You acknowledge it—"That is good, and I want more"—and that directs your hand into the bag to grab another. You may have told yourself when opening the bag of chips, "I know this is not good for me, but I am just going to have three chips." Without clarity, the thought "Yum, this is good, and I want more" compels the hand to dig into the bag for another chip until the bag is empty, and we are mad at ourselves for eating an entire bag of chips. Or, as we cultivate clear awareness moment to moment, we can fully enjoy each chip as we chew it in our mouth and swallow it before picking up the next one. By the time we swallow the third chip, we can close the bag up, feeling satisfied. We can, with moment-to-moment clear awareness, catch our hand digging into the bag compulsively driven by craving, choose not to follow the compulsion, and gently withdraw our hand from the bag. This is how our habitual reactivities can be unlearned. As we practice more, our hand will no longer dig into the bag compulsively driven by mindless craving. The habit is released, and we do not feel deprived.

The way we live our lives can be like the way we empty a bag of potato chips. Without clear awareness of our subtle habitual thoughts, we perpetuate stories that push us around in life. When we are holding the empty bag, we tell ourselves, "I don't know what happened" yet we were the one who put every single chip into our mouth. When we are at the end of our lives, will we say, "What happened? I didn't mean to live my life this way!"

If we can be right here, moment after moment with our body and mind, we will learn to recognize that our habit of reacting to the present moment with vexations causes our suffering. The more we practice, the more we become familiar with our habits and patterns, and the more we are able to see them earlier. Of course, you are always the one to decide whether you want to perpetuate these habits, to perpetuate your own suffering. We may not be able to control our circumstances, but we can choose not to suffer. If you allow yourself to reflect with honesty and practice Silent Illumination, you will realize the cause of suffering is not outside of you. Remember: *Every moment is a new moment. We may have fallen into the habit of suffering in this moment, but we can always choose differently in the next moment.*

THE THIRD NOBLE TRUTH

The third noble truth teaches that suffering can cease.

Once we've recognized how our suffering is conditioned by our unhelpful habits of reacting with vexations, we realize suffering is not inevitable. While suffering may be a default mode of our being, the Buddha discovered that it is not an inherent part of our existence. It is possible to live a fully engaged life without suffering, or at least with much less suffering. As we practice Silent Illumination, we unlearn our entrenched habits of reacting with vexation, of activating our favorite modes of operation. When vexation does not arise, neither does suffering!

We are not trying to destroy suffering; vexation and suffering do not exist as inherently, independently existing entities anyway. The third noble truth points to the fact that when the causes and conditions of suffering do not come together, suffering ceases. This is why we practice remembering emptiness and cultivating awareness of how every moment is the coming together of causes and conditions. When we forget emptiness, we reify the flow of causes and conditions into an entity with fixed characteristics. This is followed by the habit of craving what we like and hating what we dislike. The moment we remember emptiness, habits of craving and aversion are no longer fueled.

Cessation of suffering . . . sounds great! You might respond, "Yes, I want that one. How do I get that? What button do I press? What is the formula?" Well, the third noble truth is embedded in the first noble truth and the second noble truth—we need to recognize how we suffer and cultivate clear awareness of how the modes of operation that we believe will bring us what we want actually cause suffering.

You might be thinking, "I'll get rid of things that make my life miserable." That's reasonable—when we quit a job where the boss is abusive and manipulative, we do feel happier. When we get out of a hot and stuffy room, it's easier to breathe. That's likely what you have been doing—getting away from difficult situations or at least trying to. If causes and conditions allow you to make these changes without causing harm to others, there is no reason to be stuck in misery. Some practitioners insist on folding up their legs into a posture that causes so much pain they simply cannot relax the body and mind to work with the method—that is not wisdom.

We need to remember that it is our entrenched habit of reacting to any situation with vexation that causes our suffering.

With the entrenched habit of nitpicking the present moment, we can find things to hate about our new boss and work environment after the initial excitement fades. Furthermore, we may not be able to leave a difficult situation for reasons out of our control. We can't unfriend our family or quit our body. We can't get rid of everything in our life!

The Buddha discovered that even when we cannot change our circumstances, we don't have to suffer. All you need to do is stop giving rise to the cause of suffering. Remember: the present moment + vexation = suffering. If you remove vexation from the equation, there's no suffering! Just the present moment as it is. When vexation doesn't arise, suffering doesn't arise—that is the third noble truth. That is all. You do not need to do anything else. There is no need to turn suffering into an enemy to be destroyed. All you need to do is cultivate clear awareness of your habit of suffering and stop perpetuating the unhelpful habitual tendency of reacting with vexations. By seeing how the habit of craving compels our hand to dig into the bag for another potato chip, we can catch our hand in the air, smile at ourselves, and stop. Pull our hand out and close the bag. With this clear awareness, we can see thoughts for what they are, just thoughts. We don't need to let them control us. We don't have to believe in their power over us. There is no need to battle against them. When illuminated, thoughts naturally melt away like snow in sunlight.

Cessation of suffering does not mean that there will never be difficulty and misfortune. We will get sick and die, as will our loved ones. We may still encounter challenges at work and setbacks in our lives. When we face and see these situations for what they are—the coming together of causes and conditions—there is no suffering. Practicing this way is to walk on the Eightfold Path shared by the Buddha in the fourth noble truth.

THE FOURTH NOBLE TRUTH

The fourth noble truth teaches that we can cease suffering by cultivating the Eightfold Path

The Buddha taught the Four Noble Truths in the order he did for a reason. We suffer and see we are suffering, but not until we see that we cause our own suffering by reacting to the present moment with vexations can we be fully convinced there is a way to end it. People often skip the first part of the Four Noble Truths and go straight to the Eightfold Path without fully comprehending that the way to be free from suffering is to see the true nature of suffering.

Master Sheng Yen pointed out that the Four Noble Truths consist of two sets of cause and effect. The second noble truth causes the first noble truth. The fourth noble truth causes the third noble truth. Many people want to skip the first and second noble truths and go straight to the fourth because they only want cessation of suffering. This mentality is a manifestation of our entrenched habit of vexation—turning suffering into our enemy and trying to get rid of it. We need to allow ourselves to fully experience how suffering arises to truly appreciate that it is the entrenched habit of reacting to reality with craving, aversion, and fundamental ignorance that turns any moment into suffering. Otherwise, we will end up perpetuating our habit of suffering.

Remember, suffering does not exist independently. Nor does vexation. When we turn suffering and vexation into enemies by believing they are concrete and real, by reifying them, we are generating more vexation and suffering. When we realize this and release the entrenched habit of reifying suffering and vexations and reacting with aversion, the causal chain that leads to suffering is broken. When vexations do not arise, suffering ceases. The cultivation of the Eightfold Path, the fourth noble truth, is about realizing the true nature of suffering and its cause, and it can only be done properly when we recognize, face, and accept the ways in which we suffer and cause our suffering.

Seeing our true nature does not mean just saying, "Everything is empty. It is all impermanent," but experiencing it fully and in the process seeing that it is not a fixed entity. As we do, we are able to see clearly how our habitual tendencies unfold and how we are truly interconnected—we have a choice not to invest in the next thought. This is different from the way we tend to be. Very often we sit in meditation dismissing our suffering or hating it, and do not see the relevance of or the connection between what we are doing and the Eightfold Path.

And in fact, as you shall see, they are intimately related: samsara is nirvana.

THE EIGHTFOLD PATH AND OUR MODES OF OPERATION

The Buddha taught that to end suffering we must practice the Eightfold Path. It is traditionally presented as a list:

1. Right view
2. Right intention or thought
3. Right speech
4. Right action
5. Right livelihood
6. Right effort or diligence
7. Right Mindfulness
8. Right Concentration

One way to approach these eight aspects of the path is illustrated in the following diagram:

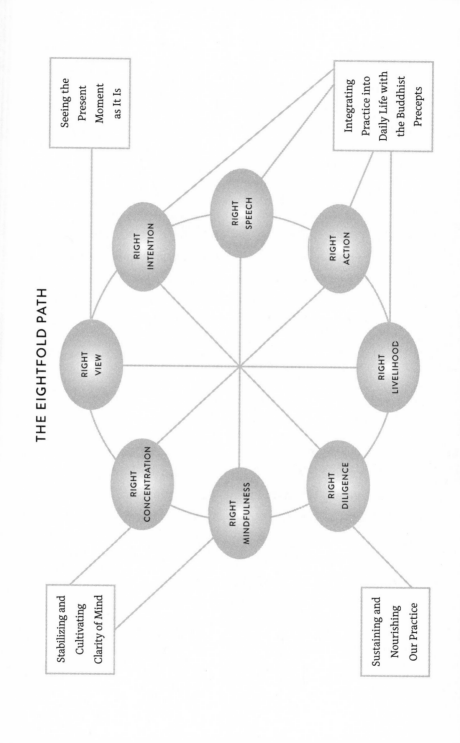

THE EIGHTFOLD PATH

Seeing the Present Moment as It Is

Integrating Practice into Daily Life with the Buddhist Precepts

RIGHT INTENTION

RIGHT SPEECH

RIGHT ACTION

RIGHT VIEW

RIGHT LIVELIHOOD

RIGHT CONCENTRATION

RIGHT MINDFULNESS

RIGHT DILIGENCE

Stabilizing and Cultivating Clarity of Mind

Sustaining and Nourishing Our Practice

I present the Eightfold Path in this way because breaking it into discrete or separate steps is not always useful. Each of the elements is mutually supportive of and interconnected with all the others—it is the eight*fold* not eight-*step* path. It is not a menu of eight items from which you pick what you'd like to do and ignore the others. If you skip one part and focus solely on another, while you may experience some benefits, you are not on the path to cease your suffering. If you are not careful, you may be inadvertently perpetuating vexations and causing more suffering for yourself and others. Recent research on the negative effects of focusing only on mindfulness without cultivating other aspects of the path is a case in point.[11] Very often, as we sit in meditation, we do not see the connection between our practice and the Eightfold Path and are unaware that they are intimately related. So, let's start there, with becoming aware—right view.

RIGHT VIEW:
UNDERSTANDING REALITY AS IT IS

Perhaps it is helpful to clarify what *right* means in the Eightfold Path. *Right* here is not used in the sense of "I am right and you are wrong," as in an intellectual argument. "Right" refers to that which is in accordance with wisdom and compassion and which frees us from suffering. Wisdom is not giving rise to vexations that cause suffering. When we are not consumed by our suffering, we are less prone to cause harm to others and are more available to bring benefit to others. This is compassion.

Cultivating right view is crucial to unlearn the unhelpful habit of suffering. Right view refers to seeing reality as it is, without distortion by our craving and aversion. Buddhists use two concepts to describe reality as it is: conditioned co-arising and the law of cause and effect. Conditioned co-arising refers to the fact that every moment is the coming together of many causes and conditions, which are in turn conditioned. If we take a moment to reflect on all that makes this moment of our existence (body, mind, environment) possible, the fact that everything and everyone is interconnected would become obvious. The moment we remember right view, our sense of separation and isolation from others that causes us so much suffering and compels us to act in harmful ways dissolves. The law of cause and effect helps us understand that what happens in this moment is not random but the effect of past actions. Remembering the law of cause and effect also allows us to see clearly that what we do with our mind in this moment affects future moments. If we succumb to our entrenched habit of reacting with hatred, for instance, we are strengthening the habit, and hatred is more prone to arise in future moments. Remembering cause and effect allows us to accept responsibility for our current situation and to commit to not perpetuating our unhelpful habitual reactivities. Our entrenched habit is to forget right view, believing that we and others are fixed entities and fantasizing that we can be exempt from the law of cause and effect. Our practice is to recognize when we have fallen into erroneous view and practice remembering right view.

It is with right view that we appreciate how the present moment—the experience of body and mind in this space—is not a problem but rather the coming together of causes and conditions. What the mind experiences in meditation is the effect of the previous moment. What we often see as a problem, such as a busy mind, is really the echo of what was going on in our life before we sat down to meditate. So, if we had a hectic or upsetting day, when we meditate thoughts will come through. We tend to treat this busy mind as a problem, and this gives rise to aversion, but it is the aversion not the busy mind that is causing our suffering.

Right view is allowing all of those causes and conditions to co-arise, knowing every moment of our experience is their merging. This includes our physical selves and the environment. For example, if you have been neglecting your bodily needs and haven't been eating well or getting enough rest or fresh air, then your mind will feel lethargic. When you are in an environment that is chaotic or uncomfortable, you will naturally experience a mind that is a bit scattered. Or when you hear disturbing news on a stressful day, you are likely to feel agitated. When you meditate and notice this lethargic, scattered, or agitated mind, you can apply right view to remember that it is the coming together of causes and conditions. There's nothing wrong with the mind. Right view allows us to not fall into the unhelpful habit of giving rise to aversion to the present-moment experience of the mind.

Conversely, when you are in an environment with less sensory stimulation, such as a silent meditation retreat, without social media or even conversation, where you don't have to make choices about when to sleep or what to eat, you may experience a quieter mind, with fewer agitating or confusing thoughts. If you believe your mind should feel this way all the time and cling to this experience, you are forgetting right view.

Remember, even the mind that is settled and simplified is impermanent! This state is not something to be attained. Rather it is an opportunity to see emptiness—how the teachings of cause and effect and conditioned co-arising manifest moment to moment. Emptiness does not mean nonexistence. We deepen our understanding of the true nature of our being— that everything exists, but temporarily. There is no independent, inherent essence in any phenomenon, including our sense of self. Every moment of our existence is the coming together of causes and conditions, the interactions between body, mind, and the environment.

Likewise, when you cultivate right view, you become more able to give rise to gratitude. It is not an artificial gratitude, where you pretend or try to be grateful, but a natural feeling because you realize how many causes and conditions make every moment possible. Seeing this is amazing! And it is the opposite of the toxic habit of taking this present moment for granted. Similarly, right view is an attitude of humility that is different from "I already know what is going to happen." We do not know. We may be able to guess, but we never really know. We live in this space of not knowing and humility when we remember that every moment is truly brand-new, reminding us to cultivate clear awareness, to pay attention to this emerging present moment.

Through right view, we understand the importance of beginning, staying with, and returning to the practice of Silent Illumination, even though that is not our existing tendency. Instead of allowing the present moment, we tend to worry about it, trying to control or ignore it. Working with right view reveals our habitual stubbornness. We want to keep doing what we have been doing because we've been emotionally invested in our habits of mind, or we are familiar with them, even though they may be unhelpful and cause us and others a lot of suffering.

In each moment we practice, we integrate and apply right view and through right mindfulness and right concentration, see that this moment is the result of the prior moments, and our response to this moment shapes the next moment.

RIGHT MINDFULNESS AND RIGHT CONCENTRATION

Right mindfulness refers to remembering to practice and to integrate right view as we experience each emerging present moment in total clear awareness. It means allowing everything into awareness through right view—being clearly aware of how bodily sensations, actions of mind, and what is going on in our environment are the coming together of causes and conditions. Right mindfulness also involves being clearly aware of the effect our actions and thoughts have on others.

This is very different from the idea some people have about meditation as emptying your mind or maintaining a particular state. If you have an idea or image of how your mind is always supposed to be, you are disregarding right view and the practice. Right mindfulness involves noticing this erroneous view and remembering the teachings of cause and effect and conditioned co-arising. If you think thoughts are problems because you believe that emptiness means that the mind is supposed to have nothing in it, and you try to block the thoughts or push them away, this is forgetting right view and is not right mindfulness.

Right mindfulness and right concentration go hand in hand. Right concentration is the cultivation of the capacity to maintain contact with each emerging present moment, moment after moment, and to reconnect with the practice when the mind drifts off. We train the mind to find a gentle presence of attention that allows us to stay here with each fluid, dynamic, emerging, present moment—without holding on to anything so tightly that it generates tension. *Stay with that just as that.* In our daily life, when we think about concentration, we believe we know how to do it—we focus hard on one task or goal by completely blocking out everything else. When we engage in an activity with a narrowed focus—perhaps reading, cleaning, or exercising—we do not notice the world around us. We have limited our awareness and blocked out thoughts and feelings. This fosters a tense state of body and mind; it is exhausting and not sustainable.

Right concentration, on the other hand, is what occurs in the practice of Silent Illumination. You begin with a relaxed body and mind. It is not forced, tense, or fixated on one point. The practice is founded on relaxation. If the mind drifts, it is not a problem; make use of it as an opportunity to practice remembering to reconnect with the direct experience of the body and mind as they are. When we apply the mind in right concentration, it is sustainable and we can function this way all day long without becoming tense. The mind is clearly aware of what is going on and not easily distracted, and when distracted it can return to the task at hand without generating unnecessary tension.

Together, right mindfulness and right concentration are the cultivated practice of total clear awareness—in meditation it is fully experiencing whatever is going on in the body and arising in the mind and seeing how we generate our suffering with our habitual reactivity. Being in this place readies us for the other aspects of the Eightfold Path, a complete package of interdependent elements of our practice. If we neglect the other elements, whatever we are doing in our meditation will be in some way misguided.

RIGHT INTENTION, SPEECH, ACTION, AND LIVELIHOOD

The Eightfold Path is at its essence about how to live a life that is in accordance with wisdom and compassion. The elements of right intention, speech, action, and livelihood help us do just that. They are directly connected to the study of the Buddhist precepts, the ethical guidelines for our lives that advise us to refrain from killing, stealing, lying, engaging in sexual misconduct, and becoming intoxicated. The precepts are crucial. When the Buddha was dying, his students were distressed. One asked him, "What are we going to do without you?" and he replied, "Follow the precepts as your teacher." The core principle of these ethical guidelines is to refrain from causing harm and to bring benefit to others. When we do things that cause harm to ourselves, that is not wisdom. When we do things that cause harm to others, that is not compassion.

Right intention refers to a mind that is in accordance with wisdom and compassion. You see, it is not so much about controlling what thoughts enter your mind but how you respond to them. How we engage with our thoughts in meditation shows up in all aspects of our lives. We remember that just because we have a thought doesn't mean we allow it to become speech or action.

Right intention is sometimes translated as "right thought." This causes confusion for some people because it gives rise to a belief that says, "These thoughts that keep coming up are the *wrong* thoughts," which leads us to try to remove or change them because they're supposed to be "right" thoughts. This incorrect understanding motivates many practitioners to block out thoughts deemed unacceptable. In the practice of Silent Illumination, whatever arises in the mind, we let through, let be, and let go, regardless of what it is.

The cultivation of right intention can be understood as what is expressed in the vow to benefit all sentient beings. This may sound overwhelming, but it is quite doable when we remember this advice from Master Sheng Yen: "Wherever you go, whether or not you benefit from being there, let that place benefit from your being there." We may resist taking this advice if we believe it means we should sacrifice our happiness so that others can be happy and feel resentful as a result. *That would be forgetting right view.* When we remember that we are all interconnected, bringing benefit to a place will inevitably benefit us because we are part of the whole. When we stop obsessing over whether others are giving us what we want (which is a form of tension in the mind), we can relax into the emerging present moment and, with the clarity cultivated from right mindfulness and right concentration, recognize how we are truly interconnected.

After all, when we are happy and feel loved and supported, we are more loving and generous toward everyone, including ourselves. Remembering our interconnectedness, contributing to the benefit of all makes perfect sense, and we are motivated to be fully present to identify the appropriate ways to benefit everyone. Right intention is giving rise to great compassion for all, including ourselves, as we integrate right view, right mindfulness, and right concentration simultaneously. It is not forcing ourselves to sacrifice our happiness for others and feeling resentful and aggrieved. These wholesome thoughts arise because they are in accordance with wisdom and compassion. Our underlying motivation for our thoughts, words, and actions, and for our practice, becomes *to benefit all sentient beings.*

Right intention keeps us from getting stuck in a place of spiritual materialism—seeking to acquire awakening or to compete to be the most generous or compassionate person or to add blissful meditative experiences to our résumés. With right intention we are practicing *not* falling into this self-centered attachment. By remembering that gaining meditative experience is not the reason for practice, it becomes easier to stop perpetuating the habitual tendencies that were motivated by a desire to create a certain mind state. The motivation becomes to unlearn these unhelpful habits that get in the way of our being fully here in the present and our ability to clearly see the unfolding of our habitual tendencies. As a result, we can stop perpetuating these tendencies in this moment and cease the creation of suffering. When we are not suffering, we will see no need to inflict harm on others. Compassion arises naturally.

The right intention of wanting to benefit sentient beings will help us remember to be mindful of the effects our actions have upon others. In some moments we might choose to perpetuate these habits, with the misguided belief that "it's just me and so what if I suffer?" But remember, when we suffer, we are more prone to generate harm to others; thus it's not just about whether you suffer or not. Perpetuating your suffering is not wisdom, nor is it in accordance with compassion.

When we pay attention to the kinds of thoughts that show up in our minds, we can engage in right speech, refraining from lies, harsh speech, divisive words, and frivolous chatter in our social interactions. Instead, we can use our speech to share useful information, to encourage and support, and to foster connection, love, and trust. Think about all the times you have allowed hateful thoughts to materialize into harsh words, the times when you have said whatever showed up in your mind, just blurted it out, and caused hurt feelings or unnecessary conflict, or when you have lied to benefit yourself at the expense of others. Cruel words and deception are neither wise nor compassionate. We can also begin to believe our lies, which means not only are we deceiving others, but we are also deceiving ourselves. Likewise, we can begin to believe our cruel self-talk, which means we are harming ourselves. In allowing ourselves to engage in not-right speech, we are reinforcing our habits of generating suffering for ourselves and others.

Right mindfulness helps us remember right view and right intention. Right view reminds us that the present moment is cocreated by everyone involved and blaming one thing or one person as the sole cause of a situation to justify our anger is an erroneous view. Right view also reminds us that the compulsion to react with aversion is the effect of a lifetime of perpetuating the habit of reacting with vexations. Clarity arising from right concentration and right mindfulness of all that is going on—the situation, its emptiness, our entrenched habit of reactivity—allows us to recognize that it is wise and compassionate to engage in right speech, right action, and right livelihood. Every moment we choose not to enact hateful or greedy thoughts through speech and action—in our daily lives and in the way we earn our livelihood—is a moment we are not generating suffering.

Practicing this way, we can live our lives—vote, parent, teach, love, or care for our planet—in a way that reduces harm and brings benefit to all. As the author Annie Dillard famously said in *The Writing Life*, "How we spend our days is how we spend our lives,"[12] and this goes not just for our right livelihood as work but for families, friendships, and all of our relationships—our interactions with people and our planet. Moment after moment, we practice paying attention to our thoughts, speech, and action and their effect on others and ourselves, along with unlearning our habits of intentionally or inadvertently causing harm to others and ourselves. As suffering arises less often, we can live more in accordance with wisdom and compassion.

RIGHT DILIGENCE

Right diligence is a commitment to practice and to the Eight-fold Path. It means returning again and again to right view and the present moment, cultivating mindfulness and concentration, noticing habitual reactivities arising, and making the commitment to stop perpetuating them before they become harmful speech, action, or livelihood. We ceaselessly cultivate this moment-after-moment, total clear awareness of our body and mind in this space, no matter where we are and what we do. We know clearly when we are engaging life in ways that are not in accordance with wisdom and compassion. When we notice this, we commit to not giving rise to more of it. And when unwholesome intention, speech, and action have already arisen, we commit to stopping them as soon as possible, clearly knowing that each moment we can choose to not give rise to the next thought necessary to perpetuate an unhelpful habit.

Everything we do—sitting, walking, working, talking,

eating, resting, sleeping . . . everything—is Chan practice because Chan is daily life. Chan is not only sitting meditation. Just as the Buddha is not to be found in a particular form, Chan practice is not to be found in any particular form. Everything is practice. So right diligence is remembering that every activity, every moment, every breath is an opportunity to practice. Right diligence is coming back to the practice moment after moment. When the mind is calm, we practice cultivating awareness of our tendency to attach to the calmness. When the mind is vexed, we see it as an opportunity to understand the subtle ways in which our entrenched habits are triggered and unfold, and to unlearn these habits. It's all practice and we do not give up. Maintaining this attitude is right diligence.

Many people think of diligence as "I do a lot of retreats, study, and meditation," putting in a huge amount of effort hoping for some visible and quick results. But that is not right diligence. Right diligence is staying present with ourselves moment after moment as we do our best to not repeat the mistakes we've made. As we practice this way, we notice our habits of mind earlier and earlier. In the beginning, you may not even know an action has harmed others, but as you begin to practice, you catch unwholesome thoughts arising before they turn into speech or action. You notice you are about to say something hurtful and stop before those words come out of your mouth because you are aware. As you commit to practice, reactive thoughts that are unhelpful arise less often because you have not been feeding them, strengthening them, perpetuating them. You become less and less likely to accumulate unwholesome, unhelpful, destructive thoughts and habits that would eventually come out in speech and action.

In meditation, when you are fully present with the body and mind in this space, stay with the practice. When the mind has drifted off, disconnected from the direct experience of the present moment, it's not a problem. Use it as an opportunity to practice finding your way back to the practice, to reconnect with the present moment as it is. When things are going well in your life, remember impermanence while you enjoy each moment fully. When the challenges of life seem overwhelming, stay with each moment and allow everything to be experienced fully and do what needs to be done within your ability, while remembering impermanence and interconnectedness. This is right diligence.

ALLOW SUFFERING TO CEASE

The Eightfold Path shows us how to live a fully engaged life without suffering. Every moment presents an opportunity to choose differently—to not follow our entrenched habit of reacting with vexations.

Often in meditation people cultivate awareness of bodily sensations and what is going on in the mind, then stop there. That is neither Chan nor Silent Illumination. You need to have awareness of everything that is going on not just in your body and mind but in the world around you. You might think that practicing means ignoring the world and isolating yourself from life's distractions, but remember: Chan is daily life. We need to allow everything into awareness to fully engage in life.

We also need to be aware of the effect of our actions on others. When we think, "I am aware of how I feel, and I am aware of what is in my mind, so I am practicing," we are misguided. When we believe the practice only involves paying attention to our body and mind, we forget the right view of our inter-connectedness. It is important to be aware of the effect of our thoughts and opinions, decisions, words, and actions and their ripple through our lives and the world. We practice to allow everything into our awareness as it is. Otherwise, our practice is incomplete. In fact, it will become totally self-absorbed. That is not what the Eightfold Path teaches. When we embody all eight aspects of the Eightfold Path simultaneously, we are not giving rise to the cause of suffering by perpetuating the imagined separation between ourselves and the world. We realize that all is thus, and suffering ceases.

THE MODES OF OPERATION

The practice of Silent Illumination is exactly the cultivation of the Eightfold Path: it is about being with what is occurring, wholly recognizing how we react to the present moment, and it is about unlearning the habitual tendencies that give rise to vexation and run our lives without our awareness, similar to the way a computer operating system functions in the background. As I mentioned earlier, I call these our *modes of operation*—the entrenched habits that we have been using in reaction to the present moment.

When vexations do not arise, suffering ceases. Clear awareness of how vexations arise is crucial for unlearning them. This is why the rest of this book will focus on the many ways our modes of operation show up and how we can become aware of them. They are how we get in the way of ourselves—our many patterns of craving and aversion, of forgetting the Eightfold Path—and how we contribute to our own suffering and the suffering of others, which, as we now know, is the second noble truth. Although these tendencies, vexations, and habits do not only happen when we are sitting on a meditation cushion, it's easiest to get familiar with them when we are doing so. This is because even when we are meditating, we are still reacting to all kinds of situations the way we habitually do, just as when we go about the rest of our life.

We can see our modes more clearly in meditation because it is a simplified environment, and many people discover their modes of operation through the process of learning how to practice meditation. In meditation, all we are asked to do is to sit and allow the body to breathe on its own. The body breathes, and there's no problem. However, *we* turn it into a problem and create suffering. The ways we turn it into a problem are our different modes of operation that are all different manifestations of either aversion or craving. Some of the popular modes of operation among practitioners are falling into a trance, problem-solving, craving meditative experience, turning thoughts into enemies, intellectualizing, and quietism. No matter the name, they are all based on our lack of clarity about the true nature of reality—that every moment is the coming together of causes and conditions.

When we recognize our modes of operation, we begin to see that they are a series of thoughts and feelings and are not fixed entities. They are not permanent defects of our being. They are conditioned by our past experience and current environment and can be unlearned when we cultivate clear awareness of how they arise and unfold moment after moment. Understanding our modes of operation is a process of self-exploration. As we see clearly for ourselves how mistaken we have been in believing that these modes will give us what we want, we will commit to stopping. We can stop perpetuating these unhelpful habits, stop deceiving ourselves, stop giving in to all our insidious habitual tendencies just because they are familiar albeit unsatisfactory. No one can do this for us. Only we can do it. No one can force us. We will stop generating our own suffering when we see clearly that it is wisdom to stop. After all, we can get attached to suffering when we identify with our suffering as who we are. We don't realize there is a different way of being where we can experience the joy and sorrow of life fully and not generate suffering for ourselves and others.

The Buddha pointed out that our default mode is suffering. As Simon Child has often taught, we're fortunate these modes of operation, while entrenched, are not hardwired in our brain or part of our genetic makeup. We can engage in the practice of Silent Illumination to cultivate clarity about how these modes of operation show up in our life, including in our meditation, so that we can stop perpetuating them. When vexations stop arising, suffering ceases. Everything still exists, just without suffering.

6

CRAVING MODE

Greedy for Experience

When craving arises, suffering arises. Craving mode is activated when we cling to pleasant experiences, or when we strive to create them by rejecting and ignoring the present moment. When we operate in this mode, whatever is happening is not good enough, it is not what we want. As we cultivate clear awareness of this mode of operation, we can release the compulsion to crave anything other than this moment, and when we do, we stop generating and perpetuating suffering.

Very often when I ask my students how their meditation practice is going, they tell me that their sitting meditation is not very good. I ask how they arrived at this assessment. For their meditation session to be "not good" there must be a reference point against which they are judging it. These practitioners talk about how they had an extremely peaceful meditation session in the past—sometimes years ago and other times earlier in the day—and they have been trying to return to or recreate that meditative experience.

Does that sound familiar? It is quite common. When these practitioners began meditation without any preconceived notion, they were able to sit and stay with the method. With this beginner's mind, they experienced a calm and clarity they had never experienced before. They may have felt the burden of body and mind disappear during those moments. It was pleasurable, and these practitioners believed that was how a "good" sitting meditation session is supposed to be. After tasting this enjoyable calm and relaxation, they wanted (craved) more of it. They then spent their time in sitting meditation trying to return to that experience. Instead of reexperiencing what they once felt, which can never truly happen, they are left with the feeling that their sitting meditation is never good enough. Meditation then becomes frustrating, and unless they understand what is happening, many people might give up, believing that practice is not for them. That is most unfortunate.

These practitioners have fallen into craving mode. This is a classic example of how we generate suffering. You may remember that the cause of suffering, the second noble truth, is the coming together of the present moment and vexations. One of the most entrenched vexations we give rise to is craving. The first and second noble truths describe how you operate in life when you think, "If I experience something nice and like it, of course I want more." This is why suffering is the default mode that the Buddha pointed out in the very beginning of his first sermon.

Why would craving more of what we like lead to suffering? Because every moment is the coming together of causes and conditions, including the calm and peace we experience in meditation. Since these causes and conditions are constantly changing, every moment is brand-new. If we experience something we like and spend the following moments trying to replicate that experience, we are bound to be disappointed. The new moment, the coming together of *different* causes and conditions, cannot replicate a past moment. Suffering, better translated as "unsatisfactoriness" here, is feeling that whatever is in the present moment is not good enough. This is why craving more of something we enjoyed in the past is suffering.

In fact, when we try to recreate an experience we liked, we are no longer fully in touch with the emerging present moment. We are no longer staying with this just as this. Instead, we hold our memory of the moment we liked in our mind as a yardstick against which to judge each new moment. We fail to recognize that a memory is not the experience itself. Instead, it is likely distorted—the aspect of the experience we liked exaggerated and the other aspects forgotten. When we are in craving mode, we are not aware of the difference; we are convinced that our memory of an experience is the experience we want to replicate. As we try to do this in our meditation, instead of allowing the totality of the present moment to be fully experienced as it is, we constantly compare the present moment with our memory of that "perfect meditation experience."

An analogy would be if instead of fully enjoying the forest with the sounds of birds and leaves moving in the wind, the smells of soil and flowers, and the moisture in the air, we took a look at the forest and then looked at a photo of the forest taken during a previous visit when we fell in love with the forest. The mind is moving back and forth between our experience and our memory. This is not stillness. Nor is it silence. Because we are so busy nitpicking aspects of the present moment that do not fit our memory of that "perfect" meditation experience, we fail to realize that this is a brand-new moment, the coming together of its own set of causes and conditions, perfect in and of itself. There is no need to recreate that old moment, but we can't see this because there is no illumination.

It is important to check to see if craving is one of the modes of operation you habitually activate in your meditation. Meditative experiences of stillness, clarity, peace, and connectedness are quite wonderful because they are moments of drastically reduced suffering. It is understandable to want to return there. Yet, the desire to hold on to it as an unchanging entity that we can possess forever reflects an erroneous view, forgetting that each moment is the coming together of causes and conditions. While that meditative experience did happen, it is no longer happening.

There is nothing wrong with having these meditative experiences. They can be helpful in strengthening our confidence in the method and in our ability to use it correctly. Nor is there anything wrong with enjoying these experiences. Where we get into trouble is when we forget that they are impermanent and in forgetting try to recreate them. Doing so only gets in the way of our fully experiencing each emerging present moment as it is. In our effort to replicate a past experience of how it feels to be fully present—to reduce and be free from suffering—we are inadvertently generating more suffering. We can instead cultivate clear awareness of the subtle habits of our mind that allows us to recognize our tendency to fall into this mode of operation.

When you notice this craving and find yourself wanting to return to a meditative experience, pay attention to how the longing to reexperience those past moments shows up. Notice how you feel dissatisfied with what is going on in your meditation because it is not that past experience. Recognize the habit of forgetting that each moment is brand-new, rendering your attempt to go back to a past experience futile. These are subtle habitual thought chains that can be unlearned when you stop perpetuating the next thought in the sequence. When you see each thought clearly as it is along with the accompanying compulsion to believe in it and act it out, craving mode will no longer hold so much power over you. You can stay with this just as this and reconnect with the peace that is right here, right now.

CRAVING IN DAILY LIFE

How we react to what happens in meditation tends to reflect the way we respond to situations in our lives. If we are habituated to fall into the craving mode, we can check to see if we want to hold on to pleasant experiences and try to replicate them. You may have had this experience on vacation. We enjoy these days away from the usual responsibilities at work and home, doing fun things and spending time with people we love. It is wonderful to have this time to rejuvenate and connect. When the vacation is near its end, we want to hold on to the experience we love so much. We may force everyone to do more things together than they feel comfortable doing. We may then become upset or offended that they do not want to spend more time together simply to satisfy our desire to get more out of the shared time, which can cause conflict and disagreement. The craving mode takes over our mind, and we become focused on how to hold on to and get more of what we like. We become increasingly dissatisfied with what the present moment is offering. While everyone is spending time together, enjoying the moment each in their own way, our preoccupation with the wonderful earlier moments of the trip leaves us without the total clear awareness of how everyone feels and what they want. It also creates tension in our mind, and the relaxation we enjoyed disappears. The wonderful experience we try to prolong and strengthen has been inadvertently cut short by our craving. In our mind, we may genuinely believe that we are doing the right thing, trying to create an even better experience for everyone. Without clear awareness of how the craving mode is taking over, we end up ruining the pleasant experience we so desperately want to hold on to and may even blame others for what happened.

This is how the lack of clarity of our mind causes suffering for ourselves and others. When we are aware of our habit of craving, we may still try to hold on to the wonderful experience, but at least we know we are doing so to fulfill our own desire and can take responsibility for hurt feelings caused by our actions. As we practice and become more familiar with how these thoughts and feelings arise, we will see how unwise and uncompassionate this mode of operation is. This will allow us to begin to notice the urge to hold on to an experience and to choose not to act on it. Instead, as we remember to stay with each emerging present moment as it is, we can fully appreciate all the causes and conditions that come together to make this moment possible. Gratitude will naturally arise. No matter what happens, joy fills our hearts. When it is time to go home, we take the beautiful memories with us, knowing that they are truly unique and special because the same causes and conditions will not come together again, but also knowing that they are just that—memories. It does not mean that we will not have another enjoyable vacation or gathering, but we free ourselves from the burden of trying to replicate this one. We can fully enjoy each new experience as it is.

CRAVING IN RELATIONSHIPS

The craving mode can also operate in the context of our relationships. For instance, some parents become agitated with their children as they get older. When these kids were babies and toddlers, they could do no wrong. The adults loved the excitement brought by the new child, and their every move was fresh, wonderful, and meticulously documented in photographs and on social media. Many parents lament how that period is too short, that the child grows up too quickly. Our memory of the way the child was in this wonderful period becomes like that "perfect" meditation experience we long to return to and use to judge the present moment. As the child grows, their mind and preferences grow and change as a natural part of human development. Adults operating from the craving mode might constantly feel that the child is not how they are supposed to be. It is not a rational thought—we know that a five-year-old is different from a two-year-old. Yet we have a nagging sense that the child is not behaving the way we want them to be vis-à-vis the memory of the "perfect and wonderful" child from an earlier time. Of course, we need to fulfill our responsibility by giving feedback and providing guidance to children when appropriate, but that is quite different from nitpicking them out of our compulsive reactivity as we operate in craving mode.

How we might react to children applies to other relationships as well. We may have a memory of when our marriage or friendship was "perfect and wonderful" that we use to judge the present-moment experience of our marriage or friendship, forgetting that each moment is the coming together of changing causes and conditions. Relationships are not fixed, yet this does not stop us from trying to replicate the past. When we do so, we generate suffering for ourselves and others. Our loved one—be it child, spouse, or friend—is being who they are in this moment. Instead of appreciating their full humanity as it is, we are generating the sense that it is not good enough because we are comparing the present moment with our idea of some past moments, and inevitably there will be discrepancies. We are setting ourselves up for suffering, and this is not wisdom. We are causing harm to others by making them feel that they are not good enough even without meaning to because we lack clarity of our mind's habits, and this is not compassion.

CRAVING MEDITATIVE EXPERIENCE

For practitioners who have not had wonderful meditative experiences that they can try to recreate, the craving mode shows up as striving to achieve special yet-to-be-attained meditative experiences. We may have read about meditative experiences described in books. We may have heard Dharma talks about the state of enlightenment as described by great teachers in the past. Regardless of the source, learning about what others have experienced in meditation may give rise to the thought "I want that experience too." We become fixated on the idea that achieving the described state of mind is the goal and an indication that we are successful in our meditation practice.

Thinking this way, we may believe practice is a waste of time if we do not achieve our goal of having these meditative experiences. As you can see, it would be difficult to stay with this just as this, to be in Silent Illumination, when we are concerned with whether we have achieved the desired state of mind. Instead of comparing the present moment with the memory of a past experience and being dissatisfied, we are causing unsatisfactoriness by comparing the present moment in meditation with our idea of what a profound meditative experience (or even enlightenment) is supposed to be like. Instead of cultivating wisdom and compassion, we are cultivating suffering by perpetuating the habit of craving the present moment to be something other than what it is.

RECOGNIZING CRAVING

Craving is an entrenched habit of mind. It is not advisable to assume that we do not fall into craving mode. Instead, we can cultivate clear awareness of the ways in which this mode of operation is activated. The most obvious is when we give rise to the thought "I want to experience this too!" when we hear about occurrences of enlightenment or deep meditative absorption that can happen if we engage in the practice wholeheartedly. Oftentimes descriptions of the peace and ease experienced by enlightened masters are cited to encourage practitioners to stay with the practice. If instead of understanding the teachings as an invitation to apply ourselves in the practice we focus on gaining the described experience, it is a telltale sign that craving mode is activated.

For others, it happens in a more subtle way. Many practitioners I have worked with have been told that they should not chase meditative experience; they are well aware of how such striving would obstruct their practice. These are often dedicated and sincere practitioners. When a teacher speaks about stillness and clarity in Silent Illumination, they believe that is what they are supposed to achieve to be a good practitioner: a mind still and clear. Yet when their mind wanders or is agitated, they become frustrated. While they are being earnest Dharma practitioners, it is a subtle form of craving experience. The mind is still engaging in the same action—judging the present moment with their idea of what it should be and being frustrated by its falling short.

We generate unsatisfactoriness—suffering—by activating the craving mode and perpetuating it without being aware of it. Whenever you feel your meditation is not good enough, check to see if some form of the craving mode is in operation. Awareness of this subtle and pervasive habit means you are practicing well, cultivating sufficient clarity of your mind.

We need to recognize that words have limitations. It does not matter how skilled the writer is, no experience can be conveyed in its entirety in words. Furthermore, words conjure up different ideas in different people based on their own backgrounds. In a Dharma talk attended by thirty people, there are thirty-one talks. The speaker has one talk in mind, and each person in the audience hears their own version of it. We have the tendency to believe that what we heard is "the talk." Understanding and remembering that this is not the case is an important part of our practice. Otherwise, we will fall into the erroneous view of believing that words have inherently, independently existing meanings that are fixed in everyone's mind. When we recognize this fact, we can also appreciate how easy it is for us to create our own idea of what enlightenment or meditative absorption is based on our interpretation of the teachings. We all do it because it is a function of our mind.

What we need to do is to remember that our idea of any meditative experience is not the experience itself. Whatever you imagine enlightenment to be, it is not that. If we insist on holding on to our idea of enlightenment to judge the present moment, we are moving farther away from enlightenment. It is not because we need to work harder to achieve enlightenment, it is because we are getting more in the way of what is already here.

The craving for meditative experience, the desire to achieve something in meditation, is a form of spiritual materialism. Very often there is a habit of wanting to have something to show for our meditation. I know of a longtime practitioner who attended many retreats and was a very good meditator, but at the end of each retreat it was clear that it was important for him to have something to show for his effort—he wanted to show how far he had come or be recognized for his realization.

Good meditators like this one often have a hard time relaxing into clarity, *staying with that just as that.* Instead of practicing the method of Silent Illumination, they cling too tightly, being too concerned with questions like "Am I making progress?" or "Is this Silent Illumination?" or "Am I getting close to enlightenment?" The craving for meditative experiences may reflect a well-intentioned striving for success in the practice. These practitioners desire to do the practice correctly but are focused too tightly on the idea of progress and attainment. As a result, they cannot relax into the openness of the method and find it difficult to flow with the ever-changing present moment as it is. Others crave for meditative experiences because they are seeking badges of recognition. They are more focused on collecting experiences—the number and quality of meditations practiced, retreats attended, centers visited, and teachers met. Such people may put a lot of time into study and meditation, but this is not the same as putting the teaching into practice and contemplating deeply, truly turning inward toward self-investigation; it is merely accumulating knowledge as some kind of possession to talk about to others, show off, or even hide behind. This is a common mode of operation, this craving for a meditative and spiritual experience. Yet craving anything—including meditative experience—agitates and clouds the mind. It is not Silent Illumination.

This tendency to crave and to attach to pleasant meditative experiences is strong. When we allow ourselves to attach to any sort of meditative experience, we are perpetuating a craving mind and vexations. You may think, "My mind got really calm in meditation, and I want more of this calmness." Instead of freeing yourself from suffering, however, you are actually perpetuating the habit of craving and generating more suffering.

CRAVING MORE OF
WHAT MAKES US HAPPY

The need to provide for ourselves and our families motivates us to work hard and sometimes we achieve success. It feels wonderful when we succeed in our pursuits and earn recognition. After you taste the sweetness of success, however, do you crave more of it the same way you crave more of the blissful meditation experience you once had? Remember, craving more of what we experienced in a past moment, such as success, blocks us from being fully here in this emerging present moment, and that is suffering. This does not mean it is bad to achieve success, but our entrenched habit of craving often turns it into suffering. Success in achieving wealth, status, and influence need not be an obstacle in our practice as long as it is done ethically while also remembering that "success" is the coming together of causes and conditions and is impermanent.

We tend to think of success as a thing we achieve and something we should be able to keep. We often let it define who we are—a "successful" person. This mentality turns success into a burden; we crave more recognition to prove that we are still successful. This idea of success as a fixed entity to possess is an erroneous view and in stark contrast to how Vimalakirti, the wise and wealthy Buddhist lay practitioner featured in the Vimalakirti Nidesa Sutra (circa 100 c.e.), an important sutra in Chan, viewed his success. He fully acknowledged all the wonderful things in his life—a wife, children, a magnificent home, respect in the community—and appreciated them as part of his Dharma joy by correctly seeing them as they were: empty of independent existence and impermanent.

Success, like all phenomena, is the coming together of causes and conditions. It involves everything that made our talent, training, and experience possible, including the physical and emotional nurturing by others and institutions that organized the social setting for us to develop, along with us happening to be in the time and space where our skills and knowledge are needed and valued. The coming together of these conditions and our effort allows us to be put in positions of authority and influence. The world considers this success.

When we find ourselves in this situation, we can make use of the convergence of factors in the moment to offer ourselves to benefit the world.

After all, when we remember our interconnectedness, we know that the skills and experience that culminate in our success are cocreated by everyone. We also recognize that the phenomenon called "success" is impermanent. Our skills and talents may be recognized as valuable now but may be seen as obsolete later. It does not mean we are obsolete as a person; it just means that our time to contribute to the group by using these skills has ended. We can contribute our talents elsewhere or contribute to the group in other ways by developing new skills. When we respond to change this way, we don't generate unnecessary suffering for ourselves and others.

We get into trouble when we mistakenly believe that we can recreate and hold on to the recognition we received at an earlier time. Forgetting that the recognition of our achievement was the coming together of causes and conditions, we suffer when things change and someone else takes over the position of influence. In fact, when causes and conditions change, it is natural that someone with different skills is required or recognized as suitable for the role we have been playing or that our position is no longer needed. Causes and conditions are constantly changing. For instance, we may no longer have the necessary skills to be recognized as exceptional or even relevant. We may have worked hard on the things that are no longer valued. We may have lost the support of others. When we maintain clear awareness of a changing situation as a changing situation instead of busying ourselves with holding on to our past "success," we can see how best to remain relevant and useful and perhaps recognize the right moment to undertake other opportunities and be at peace.

There is nothing wrong with experiences, people, or things that make you happy—it's perfectly natural to enjoy them— but craving mode actually gets in the way of our enjoyment. Cultivate clear awareness of how you react to enjoyable experiences and see if you are prone to falling into craving mode. For instance, if you love eating ice cream, do you fully enjoy the ice cream while you are eating it and feel content when you have finished? Or while you are eating it, are you already trying to get more of it because it is so delicious? In the latter scenario, you are no longer fully present to enjoy your ice cream. Have you been in this situation? Maybe you have been on a vacation and thought, "Oh, this place is awesome," and then in the next moment began plotting how you could come back next year or retire there. In doing so you are no longer actually there enjoying what the place has to offer now. You have fallen into craving mode. While you are craving more of whatever is enjoyable you are not *staying with this just as this*, and when the vacation is over, you wonder, "Where did the time go?" and return home feeling unsatisfied.

BEFRIENDING OUR MODES

When we begin to recognize our modes of operation, it is easy to think, "I get this now!" and believe that these modes are gone for good. More often than not, this is not the case. It is easy to get frustrated when you notice your modes of operation showing up in a new form. When you notice that you are no longer plotting to return to your vacation spot while you are there, you may think that you have successfully ended your addiction to craving, only to then notice yourself craving more of the moments of close connection you enjoyed with your loved ones while on vacation. While you may feel discouraged, it is in fact a sign that you are practicing well. The fact that you notice this subtle form of craving means that you are cultivating clear awareness of your moment-to-moment experience.

The belief that if you notice a habit and let it go it will be gone forever has to do with a lack of understanding of how entrenched habitual tendencies work. Unlearning a habit is not as simple as deleting a file from your computer. Of course, in some cases, it is possible for a habit to be dropped. For instance, when you recognize a habit, you may be like a lifetime smoker who realizes, "Wow, this is really not good for me or for my children," and quits cold turkey. My father did that. Some people can end habits and never turn back, but it is rare, and even if you manage to drop one habit, another similar one may take its place. For instance, my father started eating candies after he quit smoking. Many habits have deep, entangled roots in our lives, and we have been cultivating and perpetuating them for years, even decades, so they are not that easily uprooted or let go of. Craving is like that.

The habits that propel our lives are like cars we have been driving at full speed for decades. When you take your foot off the gas pedal, does the car just stop moving right away? No, it will keep going for a while as there is still a lot of momentum and residual energy propelling the vehicle forward. Similarly, you have been feeding and perpetuating habits, such as craving, for years and maybe your entire life. Can you expect them to stop just because you have decided not to perpetuate the habit? Chances are you will still notice the compulsion of craving arising when you experience something pleasant. You will notice that in certain moments, especially when you are not really with your practice, like when you are tired or when your concentration has weakened, you are prone to succumb to the pull of these entrenched habits. In these moments, it is easy for your default modes of operation to be activated and for you to fall back into habitual thinking, craving more of what you like, striving for what you do not have, or wanting to recreate past moments of happiness. So, although you might want them to stop suddenly, to be deleted, chances are the residual energy of these habits will take some time to dissipate.

However, the moment-to-moment clear awareness we cultivate allows us to see craving thoughts arising, driven by the residual energy of our entrenched habit, so that we can choose not to follow and act on these thoughts. When you begin to identify your habits, instead of falling back into them you can recognize them and let them go in that moment. As you become more aware you will recognize habits earlier, and as you continue with the practice, your ability to identify them will improve, and their compulsive power will become weaker and less insidious. There might be thoughts like "One cigarette won't hurt me; nobody needs to know," but as these thoughts arise, you recognize them. And so, the next time something happens that triggers the same thoughts, you notice and acknowledge, "Oh, yeah, it's that habit again." You do not need to give rise to the next thought, "Yeah, I might as well smoke," and act on it.

You might notice that when something happens and a feeling of craving shows up, you recognize it, and you can let it fade without the next reactive thoughts arising. As we practice more, these vexations, these habitual tendencies, will be less of an obstacle in our minds. They will show up as fragments rather than the boulders that they are now. Then you will be able to live life with a great deal more ease both on and off the meditation cushion.

With practice, this awareness of our habits is very doable for every single one of us. Be careful, however, that it doesn't lead to hating your habitual tendencies! To crave their absence, deletion, or eradication would be to fall into the craving mode! Notice them and if your next thought is "Why do I think this? I wish I didn't . . . " know that is another habitual tendency. Hating your habits, your vexations, your tendencies means you are hating your modes, and then you hate the hatred, and so on . . . and it is all craving another way of being. It sounds funny, but we often do this, which is why the habit of craving (and the other side of the coin—aversion) is often so entrenched.

Pay attention. There is a reason why the Buddha and so many Buddhist teachers talk about craving. Do not assume you do not do it. It is best to accept that you probably *do*, so that you can open your eyes to this mode of operation and the forms it takes—some obvious, others much more subtle and insidious. That way you will be able to get to know your tendencies well and when they arise *let through, let be, and let go.*

I believe one of the best ways to let go of craving and all habitual tendencies is to make friends with them. When I tell my students this, they often respond with surprise. But I mean it—befriend them in the sense that you allow them to be there. It is the letting through, the letting be in the practice of Silent Illumination. After all, they are the thoughts that show up in your mind—your feelings, stories, theories, beliefs, worldviews, values, and desires. They are part of the present-moment experience of being you. By making friends with your modes of operation instead of hating and fighting against them, the mind is not agitated and remains clear. The clarity of mind allows you to become familiar with their pattern. You recognize them readily when they show up by the sound of their footsteps before they arrive at the door. When they show up in your living room, there is no need to chase them away. You know they won't stay long because they don't live there.

Knowing the habits well means that by cultivating total clear awareness moment after moment after moment, every time something triggers your habitual reactivities, you notice it first, and you respond with, "I notice that whenever my neighbor brags about her life, I want mine to be better and I feel inadequate." That is self-knowledge, and many people never even arrive there—they just feel inadequate and get mad out of the blue at how their life, which a moment ago was fine, is suddenly not good enough. We can unlearn these unhelpful habits by noticing the thoughts as they arise and fully experiencing the feelings that accompany them without acting out the compulsion to go down the well-trodden paths of suffering. Instead, our hearts can open and be genuinely happy for our neighbor's good fortune. We can allow our day to be brightened by hearing about their wonderful experiences, reminding ourselves of our interconnectedness.

As you develop this self-knowledge, ask yourself what conditions challenge your practice. When you are comparing, when you are hungry, lonely, tired, when you are craving anything other than what is, be aware. When you are stressed out, when you are super busy, know that those are times that you are likely to make mistakes and fall into your old habits, to default to your modes of operation. Every time something triggers agitation in your mind, discomfort in your body, or disparaging thoughts, how do you react? It is seldom simply with a word or acknowledgment like "There is anger" or "I sense frustration arising." No, it is either wanting the present moment to go away or wanting it to be other than what it is. If you pay attention, you will see how your body, your mind, your whole self resists the present moment after moment.

By making friends with craving and the other modes, you become intimately familiar with how they are triggered, how they arise and unfold thought after thought, and how you are seduced into operating in these modes time and again. As you do this, you will no longer be threatened or limited by your modes of operation. They will be like old friends knocking on the door, and you will think, "That is craving. They just want to come in and say hello. Okay." You open the door and let them come in, and maybe there is something they want to tell you like how you are wishing for something other than what is—no problem. You are here to listen and kindly bring them their coat when they leave.

RETURNING TO SILENT ILLUMINATION

When we are correctly engaging Silent Illumination, we'll feel ease and confidence in the practice; craving and the other modes of operation will come through and go. Of course, it is still a good idea to reflect and ask yourself, "What am I doing here? Am I striving for a goal, craving achievement or enlightenment? Why do I meditate?"

Master Sheng Yen translated the first few lines of a poem called "Faith in Mind" by Master Sengcan (the third ancestor in Chan Buddhism who died around 600 C.E.) like this:

The Supreme Way is not difficult
If only you do not pick and choose.
Neither love nor hate,
And you will clearly understand.
Be off by a hair,
And you are as far apart as heaven from earth.[13]

Consider the first two lines again: "The Supreme Way is not difficult / If only you do not pick and choose." What he's referring to is allowing *everything* to come through in our mind; not picking and choosing only those we like. In our usual mode of operation we pick and choose the thoughts we like—the pleasant thoughts or the ones that fit our idea of who we are or how we are supposed to think, how we are supposed to feel: "This thought can stay. In fact, I'd like it to stay a little longer; I want it! I'll cling to it." Of course, with these thoughts also come the ones we reject: "This thought, this feeling, doesn't fit my idea of how I should think and feel. Now I am going to make you go away. You can come into my mind; you can't. You can stay in my mind; you can't." That is not silence. When you are constantly craving, judging, choosing, rejecting, or clinging, all those actions of the mind are vexations, the activation of which causes suffering. If we stop perpetuating these habits, we can then reconnect with our natural state of being—Silent Illumination.

When you practice knowing yourself like this, you are also capable of caring for others in the same way in your life. If you want to be able to love and connect with them, learn to reconnect with yourself first—fully, sincerely, honestly, and without judgment. Think about that. The words Master

Sheng Yen used in his translation are intentional: "Neither love nor hate / And you will clearly understand." He does not mean that you cannot love the people in your life, not at all. He's saying the supreme way—seeing our true nature, our buddha-nature—is not difficult. It is not difficult because it is already here in front of your nose. However, most people are so busy looking for their idea of what should be here that they can't see it as it already is and tend to ask, "But where? Where do I get it? What do I do?"

You might have been wondering, "I sit here, I do this practice of just sitting, I sit, sit, sit. Am I getting anywhere here? Am I closer to enlightenment? Am I making any progress?" And you may even think, "Am I wasting my time just sitting here? What would my friends think? I just sit here with nothing to show for it." Or maybe you're more optimistic, saying, "Hey, I think I am getting it. I'm getting closer to awakening—it is right around the corner!" These are different forms of craving—craving something you can hold on to, achievements you can show for your meditation, something you can talk about or write about or post on social media. Yet all the time you have already arrived. You just haven't realized it yet.

Practice recognizing this mode of operation and what an obstruction it is. These forms of comparing and contrasting, wishing and wanting—recognize them clearly, as forms of craving and vexations that cause suffering. Every time you bring up these thoughts, every time you perpetuate them, you are generating more unsatisfactoriness. By recognizing them, you can stop acting on them, and when you stop acting on them, you can be fully present to stay with this just as this and be freed from suffering.

7

AVERSION MODE

Making Thoughts Our Enemies

Aversion mode is activated when we turn something that is happening in the present moment into an enemy and set out to remove it from our awareness. Forgetting that thoughts or sensations are a natural part of the meditation experience, we try to get rid of them, agitating the mind in the process.

One of the most common responses to why we meditate is the desire to eradicate unpleasant thoughts that disturb us. Often people tell me they hate the angry thoughts and disagreeable experiences that come up when they meditate. Some are tired of the critical voice in their minds. They believe these thoughts should not be there. They want to have a calm mind either without thoughts or with only pleasant ones. They believe thoughts are intruders, enemies of the "silence" they are working hard to attain. Without clarity, they are unable to see that their habit of hating thoughts, treating them as an enemy, and attempting to reject them is what agitates the mind. There is neither silence nor illumination. As we practice, we see how this unhelpful habit gets in the way of our practice and can commit to unlearning it.

In sitting meditation, when powerful thoughts or sensations are experienced, we may become frustrated when the mind drifts off from a method, such as following the breath. We are habituated to blaming the thoughts for distracting us and activating the aversion mode to try to eliminate these thoughts. The carnival game Whac-A-Mole serves as an ideal analogy for what happens when we try to kill our thoughts. As soon as we eradicate one another arises, and we can become angrier, our minds poisoned with hatred rather than soothed by ease or peace.

Instead of playing Whac-A-Mole, some practitioners come up with other clever ways to eradicate unpleasant thoughts. Knowing that it is "not Buddhist" to react with hatred, these practitioners do *metta*, or loving-kindness, meditation to get rid of thoughts, usually without success. These practitioners are not cultivating loving-kindness; they are merely using it to mask their aversion. Meanwhile, they have completely forgotten about the practice of cultivating clear awareness of thoughts in every moment, even the angry ones.

Practicing this way tenses up the body and mind and is the opposite of Silent Illumination. Instead, we can practice cultivating gentle attention, allowing our thoughts and feelings to be fully experienced, heard, and seen. When we do so, we are actually listening to ourselves. Think of these thoughts as small children asking for our attention, wanting to tell us something. When the children feel heard and loved, they will go back to playing with their toys. Our reaction of trying to get rid of the thoughts is like shouting at the children, telling them we don't want them, and shooing them away. Because the children feel unheard and unloved, they will act out to get our attention. This is often why the more we try to eliminate thoughts in meditation, the more often they seem to return and the more powerful they become. When we react to thoughts and feelings with aversion and try to silence ourselves, it is a form of violence. Treating ourselves this way is neither wisdom nor compassion. We are generating unnecessary suffering in trying to get rid of thoughts and feelings that will be naturally discharged if we just allow them to be fully experienced, heard, and seen.

AT WAR WITH OUR THOUGHTS

Another way aversion mode manifests is when we take what I call the "warrior stance." This is aversion on steroids. We do not just push our thoughts away or ignore them, we declare war against them, fighting those that do not fit our image of who we are supposed to be or how we are supposed to feel. When we take the warrior stance we are engaged in a painful process, constantly trying to disown parts of ourselves. In doing so we can make ourselves quite miserable.

We might find the habit of taking the warrior stance shows up in our daily life as well. We can use all kinds of psychological terms, like *avoidance* or *denial*, yet it is the same habit the Buddha and other teachers have spoken about that has made our life much more difficult than it has to be. All we need to do is practice just sitting, just being, just being here . . . but we resist because of our entrenched habits. If we identify the modes of operation and cease going into battle with them, we can stop giving rise to them.

We must remember that kindness is the antidote to aversion. When we can be fully present and put down our weapons, we begin to understand what it means to be fully human—not in our imagination but in our lives. Suffering can end right here, right now, and the practice of Silent Illumination allows us to stop resisting reality as it is.

So many people harbor an incorrect idea of a calm mind being a mind where nothing happens, but it is just the opposite. Silent Illumination is nonreactivity with clarity of what is going on—we are fully engaged without falling for the compulsion to push one thought away and then grab another and hang on to it. That serene clarity is the moment-to-moment allowing of this just as this.

Remember the line from Master Sheng Yen's translation of "Faith in Mind" in chapter 6: "The Supreme Way is not difficult / If only you do not pick and choose." If you allow yourself to truly be aware moment after moment after moment, then you will be able to see how much you have been picking and choosing. We are habituated to pick the bits of our experience that fit our narrative, our idea of who we are, our idea about the world. When we do so, we activate the aversion mode—declaring war against thoughts and feelings that do not fit our idea of who we believe we should be.

For example, if you have developed the idea that "I am on my own, nobody cares about me, nobody loves me, and I just have to be strong," you come to believe this narrative about yourself and the world, and thus you only pick the moments of your experience that support your narrative. If people are being selfish and leaving you to pick up the pieces, you react with "See? Nobody cares about me. They are selfish." You only pick those moments to validate your own narrative. Even if someone is kind to you, you will block them out of your awareness because these are inconvenient pieces of evidence that challenge your storyline about the world and yourself because you are invested in believing that other people are selfish: "Nobody loves me. I am on my own. That is why I need to build this shell."

When you practice being clearly aware moment after moment after moment, you will notice when someone shows up for you or offers to help you. The narrative can no longer be sustained when you become clearly aware and realize, "Oh, wow, it is not true that everybody is selfish. It is not true that nobody loves me. This person really cares about me, and so does that one. This other person is kind of selfish, but there are people who are really kind."

Often during childhood we find a way to protect ourselves. What might be appropriate when we were young and needed to set boundaries may not necessarily be valid throughout our lives. We may need to find a way to survive something that is quite challenging, but then that challenge ends. When it does, we no longer need to live in survival mode. After all, how will it work out for us if we refuse to acknowledge the kindness around us? Not only do we suffer from not being able to experience kindness, care, and love, we are probably also hurting people who love us by refusing or denying their love.

This is why as we engage in the practice of allowing everything through into our awareness, not picking and choosing moment after moment, we will begin to see how we have fabricated aversive beliefs and worldviews that distort our understanding of ourselves, reality, and other people. How many of us have people in our lives we are fixated on disliking, in whom we can only see the negative? We refuse to also see and acknowledge the kind and useful things they do, and we might even have the same aversion to ourselves! We are fixed on believing, "I am useless. I am no good," and we only want to focus on what we have failed to accomplish and the moments when we have disappointed ourselves and others. We refuse to also allow into awareness the moments when we have been helpful and kind, when we have persevered through something difficult.

When we fully engage in this practice of opening our awareness moment after moment, experiencing ourselves without discrimination, without aversion, without picking and choosing to fit our existing narrative, we are engaging in the process of loosening our entrenched attachment to ourselves that is perpetuated by this habit of aversion, as well as craving. We realize that the habit of holding on to ideas that fit our view of ourselves and others in the world obscures and distorts our present experience and causes suffering.

When you are able to let go of the habits of blocking out and resisting parts of an experience, you allow yourself to be here moment after moment after moment, allowing whatever comes through your mind to be here. You experience it, and regardless of what is going on in the environment, in your mind, and in your body, you can be at ease with that genuine peace and stillness rather than the illusion of one you tried to create by blocking out thoughts.

DROWSINESS AND AVOIDANCE IN MEDITATION

One of the most common ways aversion arises in our meditation practice is as drowsiness. Perhaps you think, "Okay, I took a break from my hectic, busy life, and I will give myself an hour or an afternoon or a few minutes to be still and meditate." Then you spend the time sitting in meditation almost falling off your cushion or your chair—you can't keep your eyes open. Maybe you are wondering what the point is—should you just go and take a nap?

Or you may think, "No, I am supposed to be awake"; maybe you are frustrated, trying to talk yourself out of being drowsy. Many of us have to work extra hard to finish the long list of tasks at work and home in order to set aside time to sit down to meditate. By the time you sit down to meditate, you are exhausted. Furthermore, we associate being still and closing our eyes with sleep time in our daily life. It is hence quite common that we feel drowsy in meditation. Telling ourselves that we are supposed to feel otherwise and getting frustrated is suffering. There is actually nothing wrong with feeling drowsy. Our habitual reactivity, hating it and believing that we are being lazy, is what causes our suffering. Therefore, when you notice that you are incredibly exhausted and that fatigue is manifesting as drowsiness, allow yourself to rest instead of fighting it. Because when you fight your drowsiness, you are making yourself more tired. More than that, if you fight your drowsiness with frustration, you agitate the mind in addition to further exhausting yourself. You get stuck in a vicious cycle of drowsiness and agitated mind. For some people, it is so unpleasant that they stay away from sitting meditation. That is most unfortunate.

Meditation is not torture; you are allowed to rest when tired! There is a saying in Chan: "Eat when you are hungry; sleep when you are tired." If you feel genuine exhaustion, close your eyes and rest. Often, you will realize if you do this for a few minutes, you will feel refreshed. That is what people call a power nap. You are allowing yourself to *not try* to do anything and rest instead of fighting your drowsiness. This is wisdom and self-compassion. Try it if you are feeling exhaustion when you sit down to meditate.

Of course, if this persists, you will want to examine why. Is it happening every time you sit down to meditate? Have you conditioned yourself to think of sitting meditation as nap time? Ask yourself, "Am I truly exhausted?" If you are energetic and wide awake, but as soon as you sit down for meditation you fall asleep, this is a telltale sign that you are not truly exhausted. Something else is going on.

If you notice that is the case, perhaps your mind is playing tricks on you, and it simply doesn't want to practice. It is avoiding something. This is a subtle thing that the mind can do, especially when it recognizes, "We are here to face ourselves. I do not like that." You are trying to tell yourself, "That is what I'll have to do, but actually, no, I do not really want to do that," and you will find a way to squirm your way out of practicing by telling yourself, "I am tired" and dulling your mind to match your story. This is not exhaustion; it is an avoidance strategy.

This avoidance is a form of aversion. It is a resistance to being with yourself, to seeing what is arising in the mind. You are the only person who can see for yourself if this is the case. Check to see if it is and if so, do not keep lying to yourself saying, "I am just really tired." Then, check to see if what you are doing in your meditation practice is a reflection of what you are doing in life. Are you trying to avoid facing some part of your current life situation? Even if you are not ready to face and handle the situation, at least you are aware that you are avoiding it. Allowing your avoidance into awareness will help you see how it causes suffering for yourself and others. This realization will help you develop the resolve to stop lying to yourself and face the situation with total clear awareness so that you can do what needs to be done to handle it.

Another reason for falling into drowsiness in meditation is that you do not really believe you need to practice. If you do not see how much you suffer, how you generate your suffering, and how your suffering compels you to hurt people in your life, you will not see the need to practice. You will think that meditation is superfluous and there is no urgency to engage in the practice. Because you are just going through the motions when you sit, this attitude leads you to fall into drowsiness as a form of resistance. Remember: the practice is like a medicine to heal us from the disease of suffering. That is why the Buddha is sometimes called the Great Healer. But if you do not think you are sick, you will not see the need for taking the medicine. Not even the Buddha can convince you, nor do your practice for you. No one can. We need to examine how we are generating our suffering, and then we will acknowledge, "Yes, I need to take the medicine." If you do not believe you need to practice and you lack conviction, then when it is time for you to do sitting meditation practice, you are going to doze off. You will do anything but actually practice. Ask yourself if you have this mentality, thinking, "I am fine. Other people suffer, but I don't. I do not really need to do this."

USING DROWSINESS AS A TOOL

Because drowsiness is such a big challenge for meditators, over the years I've found several effective ways to work with it using concrete techniques incorporated into the Silent Illumination practice. They have helped me and may help you as well.

Make use of your posture. Often, your posture actually exacerbates your drowsiness. If you allow your head to bend down too much, it restricts the flow of oxygen and causes a bit more drowsiness and a duller mind than usual. So, if you lift up your head a little bit and align the head, neck, and spine by tucking in the chin slightly, you can set up the body to raise your spirit and maintain a wakeful mind.

Open your eyes. If you meditate with your eyes closed, and you encounter drowsiness regularly in your meditation, try to meditate with your eyes open. Rest your gaze on the floor a couple feet in front of you without focusing on anything and keep the eyes relaxed. In the beginning, you might find it challenging because of the additional sensory stimulation. When we meditate with our eyes closed, it may seem more peaceful, but we are also more susceptible to dreamy states as well as drowsiness. Keeping the eyes open and relaxed facilitates the cultivation of total clear awareness. You will also find it easier to take the clarity and stability cultivated in sitting meditation into your daily life because we live with our eyes open.

At a more subtle level, use the feeling of drowsiness as an opportunity to see how it is really a series of sensations and thoughts. Next time you feel what you call drowsiness, notice how it starts with a sensation—maybe the eyelids feeling heavy. You feel that sensation, and then you might notice a thought like "I am tired," and then you allow the eyelids to continue to close, and then you are asleep. You feel something, you think, "I am really tired," and then you give yourself permission to pass out. Instead, when you notice the sensation of heavy eyelids, acknowledge it: "There is a sensation." You do not need to tell yourself, "Oh, I am tired . . . let me go to bed." It is not easy to maintain our concentration when we are tired, but we can do it with practice. I invite you to try that.

What I've described above is more than a technique. It is, in itself, the practice of Silent Illumination: cultivating and maintaining clear awareness of the moment-to-moment experience of your body and mind at a much more subtle level. If you try, you will find that when you practice with your drowsiness this way, you will not be afraid of it anymore. A lot of times when we feel drowsiness, we freak out, thinking, "Ugh, I will lose control over my mind!" and then your mind scatters, and you cannot stay with the practice anymore. It is not necessary to be afraid of drowsiness. When you can see it just as a sensation like any other, then you stay with the changing sensation and notice how you do not have to interpret it as "I could lose consciousness and fall asleep." You can stay with it without fighting against it.

In this way we can make drowsiness a good opportunity to practice Silent Illumination. You can stay with the practice even if drowsiness returns repeatedly. This will help you let go of the erroneous view that you can practice only when the body and mind are in a particular state. When we are drowsy, we practice with drowsiness. When the mind is clear, we practice with a clear mind. When life is challenging, we practice with the adversity. When life is going well, we practice with being blessed with good fortune. Chan practice is life. Whatever is happening in this emerging present moment is an opportunity to practice.

AVERSION IN LIFE

The habit of reacting with aversion to thoughts in meditation also shows up in our lives. Practitioners who engage in this mode of operation, getting agitated and frustrated when they believe thoughts have disturbed their meditation, tend to complain about their family or jobs being obstacles to their practice. They might grumble about not having enough time to practice, owing to their responsibilities. In their minds, practice means sitting with a calm mind in meditation. This is an erroneous view, because we can practice being fully present with whatever we are doing.

This mindset of disturbed meditation, in fact, reflects an entrenched habit of attaching to our idea of how the present moment should be and blaming others when it isn't like that, turning them into enemies and trying to eliminate them (at least figuratively). At the end of a meditation workshop I once led, one of the participants came up to me and shared that he found the practice of cultivating wisdom and compassion through meditation to be really wonderful. Yet he also found it confusing and told me, "My grandmother loved to meditate, but she was the nastiest person I have ever met. She was always yelling at us for disturbing her." I told him that some practitioners love the peaceful and blissful feeling in their meditation so much that they see anything that disturbs it as their enemy. In their meditation, they give rise to hatred directed at their own thoughts or any disturbances in the environment. Imagine giving rise to hatred every time a thought arises in our mind! That is how to develop a hate-filled mind.

This habit of reacting to anything that is perceived as disturbing "our peace," as if peace were an entity, leads to hateful thoughts being directed at anyone we believe to be an obstruction to our happiness. Without clarity, these hateful thoughts arising in our agitated mind often come out as harsh and critical words, like the grandmother yelling at her grandchildren. Some people, when they want children to sit still and be quiet, use threatening language to silence them, even though they are doing what children do, being curious and playful. We would not think twice about doing that if we were habituated to yelling at our mind to shut up whenever thoughts arise or sounds occur during meditation. For some, these hateful thoughts materialize into physical violence. Instead of being able to fully connect with the people in our life and treat them with loving-kindness, we cannot help inflicting pain on them. This is suffering, and it is why we should not take the aversion mode lightly. By cultivating clear awareness of how this habit shows up, we commit to neither hating the habit nor perpetuating it.

Beware of the habitual thought pattern of defining those who are seen as disturbing our idea of how the world is supposed to be as an enemy that should be eliminated. This habit can compel us to justify aggressive and violent responses to our world's problems. If we are habituated to reacting to undesirable thoughts in our meditation by activating the aversion mode, we may inadvertently be reinforcing the habit of rejecting what we dislike. Even though we may believe in working together to improve the lives of everyone in our society and bring peace to the world, instead of listening to where others may be coming from and recognizing their concerns, we can develop a hateful mind toward the people we perceive as obstacles to our well-intentioned actions to make the world a better place. Without being aware of our tendency to fall into aversion mode, we may be contributing to the problems of the world instead of solving them.

AVERSION TO MORTALITY

If we are prone to falling into aversion mode when we experience drowsiness, we may also react with aversion to the body not cooperating with our expectations. Sometimes the body is not functioning properly due to sickness, and everything takes longer. Sometimes we do not sleep well and wake up with aches and pains. As we get older, we become forgetful, or we may fall due to weakened muscles. When the body does not behave in the way we expect it to, we react with thoughts such as "Even my body is attacking me," and we may view the world as a hostile place—another manifestation of operating in aversion mode. We forget and cannot see that this is a natural part of having a body. The aches and pains we are feeling serve as reminders to rest and be careful, to take care of the body. With an agitated mind, we turn the body into our enemy and direct our frustration and hateful thoughts at it. Before we know it, we are directing our frustration at people who are concerned and care about our physical well-being.

Without clear awareness of the entrenched habitual thoughts arising moment to moment, we can declare war against our body. Holding a particular image of how we are supposed to look and how our life is supposed to be, we nitpick every aspect of our appearance and life that does not conform to this ideal image. Since an idea is not reality, we will find discrepancies between the image held in our mind and the present-moment experience of ourselves that fuel unsatisfactoriness. People who consume a lot of media may develop an ideal image of themselves quite removed from the reality of their life, forgetting that media images do not necessarily reflect reality. They are often fantasies. Without being aware of this fact and the habit of falling into aversion mode, we can generate a great deal of suffering in the form of self-hatred. When the mind is agitated this way, we find it difficult to open our hearts to love others and to accept their love even when we want to.

This works from the outside in as well when this mode of operation shows up in our reaction to challenging external situations that are part of life. When misfortune befalls our loved ones, perhaps in the form of serious illness, debilitating physical and mental deterioration in old age, or unexpected death, we react with thoughts like "The universe is against me" and hate what is happening. We look for people to blame and cause suffering for ourselves and others. With the mind agitated by hatred of the situation, we cannot see how best to support and care for our loved ones, and our suffering may make them feel guilty for their condition. Imagine feeling guilty for being sick because our loved one responds to our diagnosis poorly.

Similarly, it is inevitable that we will encounter people who hold different worldviews. Even people who grew up in the same family often hold drastically different views. Our tendency to hold on to our self-centered idea of how the world should be, forgetting everything is the coming together of causes and conditions, and our habit of seeing any deviation from our ideal in antagonistic terms will leave us in a constant state of war against the world. This is suffering. When we are not aware of our suffering due to this habit of aversion, we can spread unhelpful attitudes such as cynicism or vengeance and cause harm to others while believing that we are doing the right thing. As you can imagine, this can be quite destructive if one happens to occupy a position of power. On the other hand, when we take good care of our mind and do not allow hatred to fester, we can benefit ourselves and the world.

BLOCKING THE PRESENT MOMENT

When we recognize we're experiencing aversion, our immediate inclination is to ask, "How do I get rid of it? I do not like this habit, this mode of operation." We may notice the habitual tendencies that are generating our suffering and hate them. We want to get rid of them. However, this is creating more aversion to what is going on in the mind. Watch out for it. Remember, when we try to get rid of our aversion, we are actually activating the mode of aversion. We are agitating the mind and creating more clouds to obscure the sky. This is not Silent Illumination. When we busy ourselves with getting rid of aversion, we block clear awareness of how this habit is triggered and unfolds moment to moment and that it too is impermanent.

This practice of cultivating total clear awareness is counterintuitive and quite different from what most of us have been taught and conditioned to do. Some people might think this sounds like nonsense and say, "I just won't let things come into my mind. I work really hard to control my mind. I work really hard to calm my mind, and I think you're just messing with me. You're just trying to sabotage my practice. What is going on here?" This common response is often followed by "Just tell me what I should be doing because that can't be right—to just allow thoughts to be in my mind? I really don't do anything to get rid of them? Or to change them or make them better? Really? No, this can't be."

Watch for your responses such as, "No way, I *have* to be involved. It is *my* mind; I must control it or add something, take something out, change something, or make something better." You may find it disconcerting to just let thoughts arise in the mind and allow the body to breathe without your involvement. Not acting on the urge to control your experience may feel wrong. Remember, it is normal for things to happen and come into awareness. There will be breath, and it comes and goes. There will be thoughts, and they come and go. It is part of the reality of having this body, of having nerve cells, of having a brain. Neurons fire off signals, and we experience thoughts and feelings. Whenever we see, hear, smell, or are touched by something—when you are outside, do you feel the breeze on your skin?—thoughts and feelings come up; we experience mental phenomena. That is a good thing! It means we are not dead. To be able to see, smell, and experience these mental phenomena is a natural part of being a living human being.

We make it into a problem by deciding, "Some of these feelings do not fit my expectations of what should be happening now. *This* feeling is not okay. *That* feeling is not okay. This thought should not be here. There should only be positive thoughts." This resistance to the present moment is a form of aversion, and it blocks our awareness of what is happening in the present moment. It is no different from you saying, "The wind is blowing the branches of the tree and causing the moving leaves to make a sound! I do not like that. I do not like that wind, and I do not like the sound the leaves make." Meanwhile, we fail to notice a broken branch above us about to be torn off by the wind.

We create suffering for ourselves when we attach to our belief of what ought to be happening and hate what we believe should not be here. As we react this way moment after moment, we perpetuate the mode of aversion. The practice here is to cultivate clear awareness of what we are up to. We are not talking about being passive and doing nothing. When we are not busy resisting and hating the wind, we can become aware of a broken branch hanging precariously above us and out of wisdom and compassion—not aversion—we take a step away from the spot below the broken branch. Recognize that we are not talking about just blissing out and thinking everything is wonderful as if in trance. We see clearly what needs to be done and do it without any fuss.

FEELING AVERSION TO YOUR MODES? REMEMBER IMPERMANENCE

As you meditate and as you live your life, watch moment after moment how you give rise to this mode of aversion. Become more familiar with your pattern and what triggers it. You'll likely see that one thought, one feeling, one sensation conditions the next. One follows the other.

Imagine someone offers you a plate of different cookies, and you think, "Ooh! Chocolate chip, my favorite!" And your next thought is, "I'll just take all the chocolate chip ones from the plate." And then you think, "Oh, I want all of the cookies." One thought after another . . . Pause and remember the right view that allows you to see the process as it happens. Everything is conditioned co-arising. Each thought conditions the next thought, and that next thought conditions the one after that. If you clearly see the series of thoughts and feelings and stories that you give rise to, you can allow yourself the space to make a choice.

You can react, "Ooh! Chocolate chip, my favorite!" and watch yourself take one cookie, and then a second, and as you keep paying attention, you realize, "I really do not need to keep reaching for cookies. It is my hand, and I can control it." You watch yourself about to reach for a third cookie and think, "You know what? I do not need to do this." You intervene not out of hatred, not by giving rise to aversion, but out of clarity. Thought, after thought, after thought . . . Every movement of your body is propelled by a thought. In this case it's either "One more, one more, one more . . ." or "I think I have enough; two cookies are enough." That is how we can stop giving rise to habitual tendencies, by being utterly clear about what we are doing in our body and mind moment after moment, understanding clearly and accurately the important teachings about right view.

Sometimes when you notice these habits are arising again, you forget cause and effect, forget that everything is conditioned co-arising, and you may tell yourself, "I guess I am hopeless. You know, I am an angry person" or "I am a control freak. There is no way I can change." When that happens, remember the true nature of reality is impermanence. Nothing is permanent—not even aversion! This idea that "I am going to be like this forever" shows up when you forget the true nature of reality. You may think, "Well, what if I allow thoughts to come into my mind, and a really bad thought just stays there and won't go away?" Remember: *everything* is impermanent. It doesn't matter how much you like or dislike a thought; thoughts go away. It may feel like a bad thought will never end, but that is because you hold on to it, you feed it, you bring it back over and over again. You obsess over it. It feels like it won't go away because you have been feeding and perpetuating it.

Have you ever been sitting quietly when a fly buzzes into the room, and you are really bothered by it? You want to get rid of it, but it is quick. You are not getting your work done. You are getting agitated and wearing yourself out, and the fly is still there. You think, "Oh, the fly is going to be here forever!" No, it is not going to be here forever. If it stays here long enough, it will die. It is not going to annoy you forever. If it is a smart fly, it will find its way out of the room, or you can open a window. The fly is not going to want to stay forever.

So anytime you find yourself thinking, "I am stuck with this thought; this thought is not going to go away; I am going to feel like this forever; I am going to feel lousy forever," remember the fly. Remember impermanence and right view. Remember cause and effect. When you notice these habits arising remind yourself, "Yeah, of course. This is a residual from a lifetime of conditioning, habits, or my trauma and addiction. I acknowledge this." Notice your compulsions, your habits. Watch them closely. Know that you do not have to keep giving rise to the next thought. It is a chain you can break. You can stop giving rise to the next link in the chain. When you feel hopeless and stuck, remember impermanence. Practice remembering; practice integrating right view.

Meditation gives us such a wonderful opportunity to do this. Relax your body so that you can settle into the present moment enough to be sitting, *just* sitting. There is this unfolding present moment. Whatever is happening now, allow it. And if you see yourself giving rise to habits of resisting, blocking, or controlling, that too is part of the present moment. Maintain the clear awareness of this habit so that you can become familiar with it. As you do, you will be much more able to disrupt the chain earlier and earlier. Not by hating it, not by trying to get rid of it, but by noticing it and making a choice. Every moment is a choice. What is your choice in this moment?

You may choose to stop a habitual thought chain, or you may continue with the usual habits of controlling, blocking, hating, fighting. It's up to you . . . but be aware! When you choose to perpetuate your habits, you are causing your own suffering. Don't blame others for your suffering and inflict harm on them. Doing so does not accord with wisdom and compassion because we are prone to more vexations when we suffer. Your choice has consequences.

RETURNING TO SILENT ILLUMINATION

Silent Illumination is our natural state of being in which all we need to do is let go of habitual tendencies. It is simple but not easy. If you notice your habit is to give rise to aversion (or other modes of operation), congratulations! You have seen into the second noble truth, more clearly recognizing how you have been getting in the way of yourself and how you generate your own suffering.

That is why I say, "Moment after moment after moment, total clear awareness." Pay full attention to what is going on. Then you can catch how you continue giving rise to aversion or craving. "I do not want this, I want that." Picking and choosing . . . "I do not want that habit. How do I get a different one, a better one?" Better habits, better thoughts, better feelings . . . "Why can't I be like so-and-so?" You are who you are now. You have the body you have; you have the mind you have. Do you accept that, or do you continue your war against reality? Accepting this does not mean resignation. The moment we fully accept the present moment as it is, when we are no longer preoccupied with fighting the present moment, we can see clearly what needs to be done and how to cultivate the causes and conditions to accomplish that.

When we are able to catch ourselves starting down the road of the usual habit, that catching is awareness. It offers us the opportunity to choose . . . and to choose differently from our habitual tendencies. Even if you do not choose differently, you recognize that is what you are doing. This is different from not knowing, from feeling that someone else is running your life, or that you're living in a place of blind compulsion. It's a matter of patience instead of expecting instant change or results. There is no need to hate your habits. Remember that you can always choose differently. That is how we unlearn our habits.

8

TRANCE MODE

Hiding from Ourselves,
Hiding from Our Lives

Trance mode obscures clear and open awareness in the same way denial obscures our view of a relationship or situation. Trance is a form of subtle but active self-delusion that creates a veil between ourselves and the aspects of our mind we don't want to see. It is one of the most common modes of operation among practitioners.

Many people believe meditation is about achieving a particular mind state; in the case of trance mode, they seek a calm, undisturbed, serene mind. To think this is to forget that the mind is the coming together of causes and conditions and is constantly changing. When we are exposed to a lot of sensory stimulation, such as news from our family, issues of work or the world, and our bodily sensations, we experience this in our minds, and we may refer to this state as "busy" or "upset." It is perfectly natural to experience thoughts and feelings arising.

Some practitioners fall into the trance mode because they believe, mistakenly, that the purpose of meditation is to experience a mind state of fuzzy calmness. With this belief, they fill the mind with a layer of fog to obscure thoughts and feelings and create an illusion of peace where it feels like nothing is going on. If you have ever driven through a dense fog, you may know how falling into trance mode is like. It feels peaceful at first, like traveling through thick fluffy clouds. But it is actually very dangerous because you have no idea that there is a car right in front of you and you are about to crash into it.

These entranced meditators are frightened by the idea of looking into the mind and don't want to go there. Consciously or unconsciously, they dull their awareness the way we would dim the light in the room. There is no illumination. The lack of mental activity, which one may mistake for silence, is an illusion. We are dimming the light so that we do not see the piles of dirty laundry on the floor. Noticing that we are generating a foggy mind, however, *is* awareness.

MEDITATION IS NOT ABOUT BANISHING THOUGHTS OR THE SELF

Let's start by looking at how trance mode shows up in the practice of sitting meditation. As we sit and pay attention to the changing sensations of the body breathing, we develop our ability to stabilize and settle the mind and open up to right view. Yet upon hearing the words *silence* or *stillness* in the instructions, some practitioners mistakenly believe that this silence or stillness is what they are supposed to *make* happen when they are meditating—by sending all thoughts away. Remember, there is no need to make thoughts go away. They will go on their own. When thoughts appear, they are already part of the present moment. *Let through, let be, let go.*

To achieve a state of what they believe is "no thought," practitioners habituated to trance mode develop ways to dull their awareness of thoughts. These practitioners often say things to me like "Oh yes, I sit down to meditate, and right away I drift into a state of peace. I can reliably go to my 'happy place.' It is as if my problems and the worries of the world vanish." What they are referring to is the ability to enter a trance state, to create fog in their minds. To make everything fuzzy, or if they are really good at manufacturing an especially thick fog, they find themselves so completely at peace there seems to be nothing whatsoever going on in the mind. If you believe that the goal of meditation is to attain a mind with no thoughts, you may think this is success and be motivated to perpetuate this foggy mind. That is not the practice of Silent Illumination. It is important to remember that we are not cultivating a mind with nothing going on; we are cultivating clear awareness of the entirety of each emerging present moment.

Furthermore, you may find the foggy mind state pleasant and attach to it because it feels better to obscure unpleasant thoughts and emotions from your awareness. It is important to address this directly by examining your motivation in the practice. Why are you meditating? If you look to meditation to escape unpleasant experiences, you will be more prone to dulling your awareness by generating a foggy mind. If a dull mind is what you are after, you will find you do not need meditation to achieve that. There is no shortage of distractions in our society to numb the mind. For many, drinking alcohol or binge-watching Netflix will take care of that.

If you notice you have the habit of generating a foggy mind, remind yourself that meditation is not an escape from reality. It is an opportunity to experience reality as it is—as it unfolds each moment. As we learn from the Four Noble Truths, meditation allows us to see how we create our own suffering and how we get in the way of wholly connecting with reality. Being in trance mode is a common means of getting in the way of ourselves.

HOW WE FALL INTO TRANCE MODE

As you work with trance mode, begin by examining your motivation. If you decide you want to relax and have a pleasant experience by staying in a trance, you may do so. At least you know you are deliberately creating a foggy mind and that you may not be clearly aware of your thoughts and feelings. You also need to recognize that maintaining a foggy mind will not end the habit of generating suffering.

Many well-intentioned people go to considerable trouble to attend meditation retreats. They arrange to take time off from their responsibilities—work and family—budgeting money and using up vacation time, and then, when they arrive, they sit with a foggy mind for days. This is quite often experienced as drowsiness where one's mind drifts in oblivion. They may sit in a dreamy state, reporting that there are not many thoughts, and they feel quite calm. Yet, this is neither silence nor illumination. They are busy dimming the light in the mind and perpetuating a foggy state to obscure thoughts and feelings arising as they convince themselves that there is nothing behind the fog. This is not silence. There is no clarity. They are aware of neither the thoughts and feelings arising in the mind nor the effort to obscure them. There is no illumination. That's why it's a good thing when we discover we are creating a foggy mind! It is the beginning of cultivating clear awareness of this subtle habit.

People who engage in this trance mode of operation are sincere in their belief that they are good practitioners because they are convinced that "not thinking" is what they are supposed to do. They approach and engage in meditation with an erroneous view, believing there is a permanent state of mind to attain. This is why cultivating right view, remembering that every moment is the coming together of causes and conditions, is important. Meditation practice is about realizing that this is so. Practitioners who engage in the trance mode want to create a certain state of mind instead of staying with mind as it is. But this foggy state, this mind in a trance that feels like there is nothing in it, is an illusion because there will be feelings and thoughts, however subtle, as long as we are alive. These meditators are veiling their thoughts behind manufactured fog instead of seeing them for what they are—just thoughts that come and go. There are still all sorts of things occurring in the mind that they are not allowing themselves to experience. And this obfuscation is a type of vexation that, of course, creates suffering.

Some of us fall into trance mode out of fear. Again these practitioners might tell me, "My meditation is good. When I sit, I can reliably go to my happy place where I feel calm." This is a telltale sign that they are operating in the trance mode. Remember, every moment is the coming together of constantly changing causes and conditions. The mind is busy sometimes and less so other times, depending on what is going on in life. We should be suspicious if the mind feels the same every time we sit down for meditation. This only happens if we are manufacturing a certain mind state that we associate with sitting meditation. Practitioners who do this have mastered a way to create a foggy mind that feels calm so that they do not see the disturbing thoughts and emotions that arise. Motivated by fear of "bad" thoughts, they have become highly proficient at shutting them out.

Whether they are aware of it or not, entranced practitioners, upon hearing that the practice is about cultivating clear awareness of what is arising in the mind, tell themselves, "I do not want to see what is in my mind." They assume that memories of unpleasant, traumatic, or difficult experiences will arise, and they want to avoid the emotions, such as anger or sadness, that they assume will accompany these memories. Or they believe they will see something undesirable about themselves or their situation that they have tried hard to avoid acknowledging. It is important to notice that these are assumptions and beliefs about *future* moments. How can we possibly be certain we already know what will arise in the mind?

WORLDVIEW/SELF-VIEW

Meditation is not a time to escape. It is an opportunity to cultivate clear awareness of the habitual reactivities of the mind as life (albeit much simplified) unfolds in sitting meditation. That we tend to activate a certain mode of operation in meditation means that it is likely an entrenched habit. This is how we can gain insights into our mind in meditation.

If you notice your tendency to create a foggy mind in meditation, check to see if you do the same thing in your daily life. Perhaps you think, "It's all good" and dismiss emotional responses to things said or done by others, dulling awareness of the hurt you feel. There is no need to exaggerate or dwell on the feelings of hurt or excitement we experience, yet telling ourselves that we did not feel anything by veiling our feelings behind a layer of fog in the mind is not staying with this just as this. Imagine a child who has fallen down and skinned their knee—we would not tell them they didn't feel that. This is what we are doing when we deny our feelings by activating trance mode. It is a form of self-oppression and is not in accordance with wisdom and compassion.

We can also check to see if we dodge discernment, preferring to live in trance, not allowing our mind to understand or be disturbed by thinking about what is going on. As we become aware of what happens in meditation, we learn about ourselves. And perhaps there's a part of ourselves that we don't want to learn about? If trance is our favorite mode of operation, we may notice that in our daily lives, when something is too painful to think about or work through, we manufacture fog to obscure the uncomfortable thoughts and feelings. We may find a way to stay in the fog by binging on mindless television or keeping ourselves super busy and exhausted. If we are afraid of foregoing these activities and allowing ourselves to just be with our body and mind, we may be engaging in the trance mode in life.

However, if we look directly at what goes on—how we react to every moment, to everything—our mind becomes clearly aware of both our world and our self. That is how we will be able to recognize how trance and all the modes of operation we engage in are not merely obstacles to awakening, they are keys to awakening. Awareness of these modes of operation provides insight into how we have been getting in the way of ourselves in meditation and in life, how we have been limiting our full connection with reality as it is, with our buddha-nature—our innate goodness. With this insight, we can unlearn these unhelpful habits.

When we fall into the trance mode of operation, we are limiting not only our worldview and self-view but our lives as well. This occurs because we preserve the self as a permanent entity with certain characteristics and relate to our experience of the world in a particular set way. This view of the world as being a particular way, being something unchanging that holds lurking threats or is unsafe or unfair, is a subtle and pervasive part of our self-view. Without allowing ourselves to fully experience our relationship with the world, we are not allowing ourselves to investigate what is going on within.

We need to see through the fog that is deluding us and causing us to believe that the self is permanent, that the phenomenon of self has an independent existence and fixed relationship with the world. Such erroneous views perpetuate a sense of separation, which is a form of suffering. Without awareness of the modes of operation we activate, we will not have the opportunity to unlearn vexatious habits, to see through these erroneous views, and to realize the true nature of our existence—of reality—by becoming free from the prison we have built for ourselves out of bricks made of fog.

If we ignore the mode of cultivating and maintaining a foggy mind, our spiritual practice won't develop; it will become stunted. Even though you are a diligent meditator and believe you are being a serious practitioner, without noticing this trance mode of operation, you are cultivating a foggy mind instead of clear awareness. As you'll see, often this habit shows up in how we set up and live our lives.

THE "GOOD" MEDITATOR

"Good" meditators tend to love meditation. These people take pleasure in discussing how their practice is going. They know how to enter into a calm place when they sit down to meditate. Often, they have figured out how to live their lives in a similar way—they have made everything simple and peaceful, often by avoiding anything that may be upsetting. These practitioners genuinely believe they are practicing *and* living well. Yet these people may, without being aware of it, be stuck in the trance mode of operation. They have a difficult time letting go of this habit because they believe they are *there*; they believe they've reached their meditation destination and do not realize they are lost in the fog.

Practitioners in trance mode can be kind and generous in their own way, but often they do not notice when there is something wrong. They are so invested in their foggy mind that they want to focus on maintaining it to the point of sealing themselves into it, creating a state of imprisonment to preserve the calm.

The trouble is, when someone practices this way—and they may have been practicing this way for years or even decades— it is limiting their potential. They could have engaged life in so many ways if they were more willing to connect with new people or strangers, form bonds or relationships, or engage in activities that present the opportunity to fulfill the potential of their natural talent, but they do not allow this to happen because trance mode limits their life to a small calm space.

They are also limiting their spiritual development because they are not cultivating clear, total open awareness. Encased in a cloud of fog, they are unable to see the subtle habits of the mind because they are not willing to allow whatever arises to be there and experienced fully. When they are unable to see the subtle habits of their mind, they are also not allowing the revelations that seeing thoughts—and all the powerful, pervasive, subtle habits that go with them—bring as an opportunity for spiritual growth.

These practitioners lose touch with their emotions as well. When practicing in trance mode they are hiding the unpleasant or difficult parts of life behind a veil of fog; they do not allow themselves to feel and as a result they are not experiencing life to the fullest.

Cultivating clear awareness can be quite a challenge for these practitioners. Because they believe their meditation is going well in this foggy mind state that feels calm, they resist allowing thoughts and feelings into awareness that might upset them. There was a retreatant who told me he was fine. When I asked him about his life, he mentioned that his neighbors were doing something quite egregious—leaving a barking dog tied up in the yard. Instead of acknowledging and taking appropriate action, he minimized the situation and the neighbor's behavior, even though it was quite obvious it was vexing him. This is not some trivial thing—the noise, the dog's suffering, the lack of consideration—it is all happening and disturbing this person and others.

When we dull our awareness in trance mode, we cannot empathize with those who are suffering. We may even make them feel inferior for being affected by the situation, thinking that we are superior because *we* are not suffering, when the truth is we are merely unaware of (or avoiding or suppressing) our suffering. This is a form of spiritual bypassing. Without facing the situation as it is, we are unable to identify appropriate actions to ameliorate a situation. We are prone to resign ourselves and become passive, mistakenly thinking we are a good practitioner while leaving the situation for others to deal with. In the case of the retreatant, he and his wife could not sleep due to the barking dog. He had a good relationship with the neighbors and could have spoken to them about the situation, but he did not do anything because he would not allow himself to acknowledge that the situation was problematic. After several sleepless nights, his wife, who is afraid of dogs and their other neighbors, couldn't take it anymore and called the police. It made her anxious to antagonize their neighbors by calling the police, but she felt she had no choice.

As you begin to practice Silent Illumination you will find clarity and be more able to see when you fall into trance mode when something happens at work, or when there is a problem in your relationship, or when you learn of serious issues in the world—any unpleasant or troublesome situation. Pay close attention to the tendency to create a foggy barrier to obscure your emotional response as you fall into trance mode. This barrier is a form of resistance to the present moment as it is—it is vexation and it causes suffering. Notice how you might tend to minimize what happened, and how you might be unwilling to acknowledge that you felt anything—such as anger or fear—regarding the situation. When this happens the tendency is to deflect, saying things like "That is the way it is," and become reluctant to acknowledge your emotional response, work with those emotions, or handle the actual situation.

HIDING FROM LIFE

Trance can be a way to hide from life, and as a result, when we are in this mode of operation, we may not be fulfilling our responsibilities. If there is a conflict in the family or at work due to misunderstandings and inadequate communications, our evading this conflict by manufacturing a cloud of fog between us and the situation to preserve a false sense of "it's all good" is not in accordance with wisdom and compassion. Sometimes, we may be the one who can clear up the misunderstanding that causes the conflict. By disengaging ourselves from the situation, we are not aware that this is the case and are contributing to prolonging the conflict with our silence. While we believe that we are being a good practitioner, we are actually neglecting our responsibility!

Someone told me about a practitioner who prided himself on being unmoved by situations. He oversaw an organization in which a manager was alienating her colleagues and subordinates, and the work environment had become quite toxic. People looked to this practitioner to do something because he was the manager's supervisor. Rather than looking into the situation to identify solutions, he chose to keep a cloud of fog between himself and the situation to preserve his calm because he knew the messy situation would be upsetting. Meanwhile, the manager was not receiving feedback and support from him, and the situation further deteriorated.

The people who make their lives too calm, who erase anything unpleasant and do not allow themselves to confront the deep resentment they harbor or their fear or discomfort, are not allowing themselves to look inward to investigate what is going on. They fail to ask, "What is this feeling about?" and hence miss the opportunity to let the feeling reveal their interpretation of a particular situation, which in turn reflects their limited self-view and entrenched worldview. Without clear awareness of thoughts, we perpetuate unhelpful habits of the mind that in turn shape our actions, causing suffering for ourselves and others.

Often getting stuck in trance mode occurs because we somehow come to believe that the lack of emotional response is a sign of good practice. Just as not thinking is *not* Silent Illumination, *not feeling* is not Silent Illumination either. It is important to pay attention to the process. When we believe having an emotional response equals bad practice and thus is undesirable, we may be motivated to obscure the presence of emotions or dampen their intensity with a foggy mind to preserve our sense of being a good practitioner. Doing so leads us to believe that our reactivity is mild or even nonexistent when in reality we are extremely angry or embarrassed (or are feeling other intense emotions). Because we obscure aspects of the situation that trigger the emotional response, there is no way to discern whether our anger is a natural result of mistreatment or due to unreasonable expectations. Meanwhile, the unacknowledged anger festers and may compel us to inflict pain on others, often in regrettable ways and without our being aware of doing so.

When we obscure our emotional response there is usually a lack of awareness of this action. This is indicative of the trance mode and creating a foggy mind. When we do this, we tend to really want to focus on maintaining a calm mind. And if we have any questions at all, or identify any "problems" in our practice, we usually just want to find out how to preserve or return to the calm mind and not let any thoughts disturb our calmness. In other words, we are not letting through and letting be. Awareness of trance mode allows us to notice what is driving it—usually an urge to avoid what is difficult or unpleasant in our lives. Deeply buried intense feelings can lead to a fiercer and more insidious kind of suffering.

Many practitioners do this—obscure the things they do not think they can change and instead get stuck in fuzzy, calm, blocking-out trance mind, not for pleasure or ease in their useful sense, but to escape discomfort and painful emotions. There is a strong resistance to acknowledging the underlying frustrations, the difficult and uncomfortable feelings and thoughts or traumatic experiences that clearly make a deep imprint in life. For example, a student of mine endured microaggressions and not-so-microaggressions from her boss. She needed the job and liked the work, so she buried the discomfort that led to emotional pain and ultimately emotional paralysis—she tried to hide in a fog, but ultimately it didn't work. After many retreats this practitioner was finally willing to acknowledge and voice what she was going through and to see through the fog to her suffering. It was a demanding and emotional process, but by going through it she developed the clarity to address her situation with wisdom, ultimately looking for another job and, in so doing, compassionately taking care of herself.

BURYING TRAUMA AND
GETTING RID OF PROBLEMS

The fear of facing a difficult or unpleasant situation can be so great that we can come to hate it when memories, thoughts, or feelings arise. Yet allowing them through, allowing them to be fully experienced, seen, and heard, is an important part of the practice of Silent Illumination. Recognizing that we are generating a foggy mind to deny unhappy memories means we are cultivating clear awareness. Some practitioners prefer to reject that. They often say things like "What is the point of going back to all that? It is the past, and is not the past what we are supposed to let go of? I want to live in the present." Well, how about the present-moment experience of these memories and thoughts arising?

Often people are attracted to meditation practice because they believe they will "get rid of" unpleasant, traumatic, or difficult experiences or situations. What happens is that through meditation in trance mode, these practitioners have learned to effectively obscure their troubling emotions and thoughts. They learn to meditate, picking up on only a part of Silent Illumination—their erroneous interpretation of silence—instead of the whole practice and missing out on the illumination piece. One may get so good at creating this veil to obscure unwanted thoughts and feelings that one becomes detached from oneself. Some practitioners report becoming emotionally numb. And yet they often find it incredibly useful in blocking out unpleasant thoughts and emotions. *At least for a while ...*

When it stops working, they tend to double down on their mode of operation. However, not allowing these thoughts or feelings to arise and be experienced fully often indicates an underdeveloped meditation practice and perpetuates the fear they are trying so hard to get rid of. They do not feel safe allowing themselves to experience these difficult life situations, likely fearing that if they acknowledge the pain or anger, they might explode or act out in a way that is not considered acceptable, perhaps because expressing anger brought about dire consequences in their past. This is a delicate situation for these practitioners and must be handled with great care. For many, especially those who have experienced trauma, it is not advisable to engage in this practice intensively without working with an experienced teacher and perhaps a psychotherapist as well who can provide support.

If you are such a practitioner, as you work with a teacher or therapist, you can practice noticing whether you have the habit of not wanting to see what is going on. Are you afraid to see a situation for what it is? Are you afraid to face yourself and the reality of your situation? Do you activate trance mode to dim the lights, so to speak? Underlying this fear, you may be imagining that you need to turn on all the lights at once and become overwhelmed by what is revealed. But suddenly turning on all the lights may not be appropriate for you at this point. You can start with being aware that the fog is created by you. It is entirely up to you how much you want to reveal; the process is entirely within your control. Rather than assuming that what is obscured is dangerous, be curious. When you see that the foggy mind is hiding understanding, you will naturally stop perpetuating it. It is *your* practice, and it is important to work with yourself kindly and gently.

LYING TO OURSELVES

Foggy mind is a form of disengaging from life to avoid facing the suffering caused by our attachment. Relationships and careers happen as causes and conditions come together. They don't have to bring suffering. We suffer when we forget that they are impermanent and attach to them as if they are a permanent and essential part of who we are.

A common example is the identification with our job as our life's meaning and who we are. What we practice letting go of is the compulsive tendency to crave the part we identify with and wish was permanent. We often attach to the aspect of our job that gives us power, confidence, and status, while we fear the disappearance of our influence or livelihood as causes and conditions change at work and in the larger society. Because we don't want to face the suffering caused by our attachment and be worried about how our life may be turned upside down by these changes, we tell ourselves that we don't really care about what will happen. To show ourselves that we don't care, we disengage and stop paying attention to what is happening. This oblivious attitude helps to preserve the illusion that disturbing changes are not happening. This may appear to be a good strategy to avoid being worried and upset, but the underlying aversion to change and uncertainty is still there. To maintain the illusion of calm, we have to keep lying to ourselves and generating more fog to obscure the situation from our awareness. This is not silence. Meanwhile, we don't know we are lying to ourselves to avoid discomfort and are fooled by our lies. This is not illumination.

Some people may work in a traditionally respected profession that is becoming less important with technological changes. In the practice of Silent Illumination, instead of disengaging from the constantly changing reality of the world as it is, we allow the shifts to be experienced and seen clearly as they happen. If we do this instead of burying our head in the sand or wrapping our mind in a fog, we will not feel so betrayed and resentful when we are forced to reckon with the new world. We will also be more ready for new circumstances, perhaps by noticing the new skills we need to develop as the previous ways of doing things become obsolete. When we can practice this way, clearly seeing the changing causes and conditions and our habitual aversion to impermanence, we can choose to let go of the habit of resisting the changes around us that are out of our control and free ourselves from unnecessary suffering.

This does not mean doing nothing! We may be doing many things, but they are not done from the place of aversion to the changing causes and conditions. We allow the clarity from a nonreactive mind to guide our response so that we can see what needs to be done and do it, to recognize what cannot be done and accept it, and to refrain from acting in ways that cause unnecessary suffering to ourselves and others. This is what is meant by responding appropriately as we remember to practice in each moment. Our responses are in accordance with wisdom and compassion.

There are times when driving in the fog is dangerous, and the same applies to living in trance mode. When we are in this mode, we avoid seeing what is actually unfolding in our minds, bodies, and shared human experience. The fog gives the illusion of calmness, but it is only because we can't see with clarity. Sometimes we are in such a deep trance, we avoid the truth of our lives. We risk being completely blindsided by harsh realities, like our parents dying or our marriage failing or our job becoming obsolete or the climate destabilizing. Letting go of trance mode is really about being able to stay with the most fundamental questions of being human—suffering, aging, sickness, and the death of ourselves and our loved ones.

It is very much what the Buddha talked about in the Four Noble Truths. Some people are invested in trance mode, believing that they are avoiding suffering, when what they are actually doing is causing great and prolonged suffering, which is not in accordance with wisdom and compassion.

RETURNING TO SILENT ILLUMINATION

Practice remembering to notice. When you are dulling awareness remind yourself to sharpen your awareness and reconnect with the practice of Silent Illumination—stop creating more fog. The more we practice remembering, the less foggy we'll be, and in the process, we will reveal all the habits that have gotten in the way of how we respond to life situations. We tend to get frustrated when we fall back into our habits. We may get impatient that the residual power of the habit is still lingering. Seeing those tendencies is practice, too. Whatever it is that you do, you will learn something about yourself, and that is why Chan practice is a journey of self-exploration. We are not here to learn how to be the world's best meditator or train to enter the Meditation Olympics with the aim of bragging about how long or well we meditate, proclaiming, "I can count the breath from one to ten and back from ten to one perfectly."

That is not what we are doing when we meditate. We use the meditation method to settle the mind so that we can see through the fog and see more clearly into the mind to notice all the habits that we use to generate our suffering without our knowing. When we notice we are creating the foggy mind, we can choose to begin to stop doing that. Or we may choose to *keep* doing that, but at least we know that is what we are doing. We are aware that we are deliberately obscuring something in our mind, and when we are ready, we will allow these thoughts and feelings to be seen. Without awareness, we are living in a trance. We are living like zombies. The trance mode is a form of vexation—craving a calm mind state and rejecting the thoughts and feelings we do not want to notice by dulling our awareness.

As we practice remembering to be aware and staying with this just as this, we begin to notice when we are not aware and that our mind is dull. We realize that we have been generating a foggy mind. This is what happens when we practice Silent Illumination. You will notice that your habits are quite entrenched. After a glimpse of clear awareness, you may fall back into a dreamy state. To continue cultivating this clear awareness, practice recognizing how the fear of unpleasant thoughts motivates you to dim the light of the mind. Notice that it is an erroneous view to assume that you already know what kind of thoughts will arise in your mind. Remember, every moment is brand-new. Also, practice paying attention to the belief that there are thoughts that are inherently unpleasant, forgetting that thoughts are just thoughts, without any inherent characteristics. Recognize how your desire for a calm state of mind turns meditation into an escape from life. In the process, familiarize yourself with how trance mode is triggered and activated. When you do so, you can see for yourself that what we call vexation is not an independently existing entity. It is a chain of thoughts and feelings that starts with an assumption that there are inherently unpleasant thoughts and is followed by fear and aversion to experiencing unpleasant emotions and then action to dull the mind, which triggers the sensation of heavy eyelids and fog in the mind. Allow these thoughts and feelings to be experienced for what they are—impermanent and without independent existence.

Do we need to let the fear of these fleeting thoughts take over and control us? Of course not! There is no need to hate these habits. We may notice a strong tendency to want to get rid of them, and this urge may be accompanied by hatred. Be clearly aware of such tendencies or else they will take over and generate more vexations and suffering. We work with ourselves to gently unlearn the habit by releasing the urge to give rise to the next thought in the chain. When we notice fear or desire, we practice staying with each emerging present moment and maintain clear awareness. When we notice the mind dulling down, we gently sharpen our awareness. This is the gentle effort in the practice of Silent Illumination. We are not just sitting here spacing out in the fog.

9

PROBLEM-SOLVING MODE

Trying to Fix the Present Moment

When we are in problem-solving mode, we compulsively pick apart the present moment as something that needs to be fixed. We sit with our body and mind, a thought arises, and instead of letting through, letting be, letting go we turn it into a problem even though it is perfectly normal for there to be thoughts. Instead of remembering to stay with this just as this, we busy ourselves with identifying and solving "problems." We agitate the mind by doing so and create more "problems" that need "solving." We are unable to experience the moment fully, *as it is*, amid the constantly changing causes and conditions that bring about each emerging present moment and instead try to adjust it. This is a classic case of suffering—no matter what is in the present moment, something is not quite right.

A few years ago, I was leading a Sunday meditation workshop at a center where I teach regularly. I took the group through a guided practice as they settled their bodies into the meditation posture. I encouraged them not to control the breath—to allow the body to breathe on its own. At the end of the session, I invited everyone to share their experience. One participant who was new to practice—it was her first time doing sitting meditation—told us she was shocked to see that her body had been breathing without her regulating it this entire time! She said, "I can't believe that my body has been breathing on its own all this time without me doing anything! This is a problem. I need to do something about it!" Her body breathing on its own had become a problem she needed to solve! This was quite an interesting comment, but it wasn't an unusual one. She articulated what many new and longtime meditation practitioners alike experience. Until this meditation workshop, she had been oblivious to the fact that her body had been breathing on its own to remain alive since the moment she was born. Instead of marveling at the miracle of their breathing bodies, people habituated to operating in problem-solving mode tend to automatically assume something is problematic and needs fixing once it is in their awareness even though it has been happening all along.

FIXING WHAT ISN'T BROKEN

The mode of operation I call problem-solving involves several habitual tendencies. First of all, it involves labeling or characterizing what is happening in the present moment as a "problem" and reacting to this problem by seeking to fix it. In other words, the activation of the problem-solving mode of operation automatically overtakes a situation whether there is a problem or not. It is important to pay attention to the fact that what is identified as problematic is something that has been going on that is not truly problematic at all. I use the example of the body breathing, but this also shows up in other ways, such as when people notice their heart beating when they meditate or how often they need to blink or swallow. And of course, it also applies to phenomena outside of our body, like nitpicking your child or partner's behavior at home or micromanaging at work. One student shared with me that when she did a meditation exercise with her husband, sitting face-to-face in silence, she noticed herself finding fault with everything he did even though he was simply sitting there. In that moment, she realized that all the problems she saw in her husband were the creations of her own mind.

These things—the body breathing, people living their lives—have always been going on. When we weren't paying attention, they weren't part of our awareness. When we allow them into our awareness, the problem-solving mode may be activated. So, the first component of recognizing the problem-solving mode of operation is to notice when we turn what comes into our awareness into a problem simply because it is in our awareness.

It is important to clarify that solving problems when the problems are real is not an undesirable thing. When a child has trouble learning, it is the parents' responsibility to find out what can be done to help them. When a society consistently treats some people inhumanely, we need to work on ameliorating the problem of discriminatory institutions. That is very different from the entrenched habit of characterizing what is naturally occurring and not actually a problem as a problem and compulsively activating the "fix-it" mode, which may not be appropriate for the situation. This often blocks us from staying with this just as this, allowing the present moment to be, allowing ourselves to be fully here with what is happening, appreciating the fullness of an experience. Instead, by allowing the problem-solving mode of operation to take over, we may be compelled to look for something to solve in order to occupy ourselves, which in turn keeps us from fully experiencing and seeing what is truly going on in our minds and our lives.

For some people, this may be a form of avoidance, sidestepping how they truly feel without being conscious that they are doing so. Seeing experiences as problems that need to be solved prevents us from fully appreciating what is going on in the present moment and relaxing into it. We need to realize that what occurs in most given moments is actually just fine, that it is usually not necessary to activate our problem-solver self, and it is okay for this mode of operation to take a break.

When we have an entrenched habit of being a problem-solver, it is a form of resistance to the fact that this problem-solver self does not need to operate at all times. This is particularly difficult for individuals who identify as effective problem-solvers. It is a self-concept we may be particularly attached to. Perhaps we have been *raised* to be good problem-solvers. We have been encouraged to take on this role and rewarded for it at work, school, or home. This ability makes us feel needed, empowered, or in control. Again, it is important to remember, we are not talking about problem-solving being something that is always negative—the people who design dams and bridges, who create vaccines and build hospitals, are all solving problems. But problem-solving mode is not appropriate or necessary at all times. When we allow this mode of operation to become automatic, we do not see the situation as it is, instead predicting or finding problems when there are none or exaggerating their scope.

Perhaps there is a transition happening in your life that is not going smoothly, or you are involved in a disagreement due to inadequate communication. If you allow a situation like that to be seen clearly, it will become quite straightforward, and you can understand what needs to be clarified and communicated to put an end to the conflict. However, if you habitually fall into the problem-solving mode of operation, you latch on to that natural transition or what might be a minor communication issue and turn it into a big problem, allowing the problem-solver self to take over and label the entire situation a "problem." Oftentimes as a result, everyone else in the situation will eventually be seen as a part of that problem that needs to be fixed too.

The habit of assuming that something is problematic blocks us from fully experiencing this moment as it is. Instead of responding appropriately with wisdom and compassion after gaining a clear, undistorted understanding of the situation, we compulsively activate problem-solving mode. Operating in this mode causes a lot of unnecessary stress and conflict for us as well as suffering for the people around us.

THE "PROBLEM" WITH BREATHING

Along with "My body is breathing without me!" another common remark I hear from practitioners of meditation when they are introduced to the method of following or counting their inhalations and exhalations is "I can't feel my breath." This is quite interesting because, of course, their body most definitely has not stopped breathing. Yet these practitioners believe they cannot feel their breath. When they say this, what they mean is that they are not sensing the breathing sensation that they *expected* to experience. Instead of following their breath as it is, these practitioners are looking for something else, looking for the *idea* of breath they have created in their minds. When they can't find an experience that matches this idea of how the breath is supposed to be, they see a problem. They often try to fix the "problem" by modifying the breath to fit into their preconceived notion of meditative breathing, and in so doing tense up the body, agitate the mind, and get in the way of staying with this just as this.

Oftentimes, accompanying the thought "I can't feel the breath" is the entrenched habit of judging or qualifying the present-moment experience of breathing. For example, practitioners might say that their breath is too irregular or should be deeper, and it's a problem! The keyword here is "too" or "should" instead of reporting something like "Oh, I noticed that my breathing is sometimes shallow and sometimes deep." Judging the breath and describing the breath are not the same. This is why it is helpful to listen to yourself attentively; it allows you to notice the subtle and entrenched habit of judging the present experience against a certain idea that you hold about what is supposed to be happening and turning it into a problem.

When it comes to the breath, there may be an underlying expectation that the body is supposed to operate like a machine with muscles contracting and relaxing at fixed intervals without any variation. It is an odd idea, but in this day and age, we increasingly perceive human beings like machines. Check to see if you have subtle thoughts or ideas like these that motivate you to make judgments and comment on a perceived inadequacy or flaw in your meditation, characterizing and turning it into a problem. Then, ask yourself, "Is there really a problem?" Practice remembering right view. Your body is breathing the way it is breathing in this moment within the causes and conditions that have come together. This may have to do with the air temperature, humidity, your health, and so forth. Relax into each emerging present moment as it is and stay with this just as this. You will realize that the body is breathing the way it is breathing in this present moment, and it's not a problem.

When you fall into problem-solving mode and see the breath as a problem, the problem-solver self is activated automatically because the habit is so entrenched. And often, without our knowledge, we try to fix or adjust the breath to be the way we think it is supposed to be, solving a problem where there is none. The most common way meditators use to "solve the problem" is to control the breath. In fact, controlling the breath is one of the most common issues for practitioners who settle the mind by following their breath. Instead of allowing the body to just sit and breathe on its own, we get in the way of the present moment. If you have done this, you will recognize that controlling the breath creates tension because you are not allowing the body and mind to relax. In fact, for many people, the tension actually increases as they meditate this way, and they become frustrated because they were hoping to relax their body and mind through the practice. You'd be surprised how often I hear people complain that meditating with the breath is stressful! Some say they feel the tension in the chest area, others might become anxious if the breath seems to be getting shallow—whatever it is, it often has to do with the fact that they are controlling the breath.

Often practitioners control the breath because they want their meditation to be perfect. Upon hearing the instruction to use the breath method to settle the mind, they assume their job is to follow each inhalation and exhalation perfectly and deem anything else as a problem! They are likely to see drifting off from the method as a form of failure. They may see the wandering mind as a problem when it is not really a problem. The mind wanders sometimes. That's what it does. The practice is to cultivate clear awareness of the moment-to-moment experience of mind. That is why, when I lead guided meditation, I often remind practitioners that it doesn't matter how often your mind drifts off—as long as you can find your way back to your method, you are practicing well.

For practitioners who want their meditation to be perfect, the thought process is often something like "My mind keeps drifting away from my breath, it's a problem and I need to solve that problem! How do I go about it?" Controlling the breath may seem the obvious solution because if I control the breath, I choose when to exhale and inhale. Then voilà! I solve the problem of drifting off the breath because I know exactly when exhalation will happen since I am the one who makes it happen. There is no way for me to miss the moments of inhalation and exhalation. Problem solved!

There are also practitioners who incorporate counting from one to ten into the breathing method. They find it particularly effective to stabilize the mind. For them, the "problem" is losing track of the count. Again, when you are the one who controls when exhalation happens, of course you can count each exhalation. You will be able to count from one to ten perfectly. There are practitioners who report to me that their meditation is going well because they can reliably count from one to ten and can feel the breathing consistently. When I've encouraged them to look into it, they realize what they have been doing is controlling their breath—not cultivating clear awareness.

Sometimes this is because they believe that is what they are *supposed* to be doing. This is especially true for some people who have a yoga practice—they might have confused Chan practice with other kinds of meditation practice in which one is encouraged to regulate the breath in a deliberate way. In the Chan practice of Silent Illumination, we let the body and mind be, allowing breath to naturally occur on its own. This is why it is a good idea to check with an experienced teacher even when you believe your meditation is going well.

UNCERTAINTY AND CONTROL

When we recognize that we are falling into problem-solving mode, it gives us an opportunity to see our underlying habit of resisting reality as it is, generating suffering for ourselves and others. Seeing the variation in the rhythm of the breathing as a problem and solving it by controlling the breath is often motivated by our fear of uncertainty. It is a common fear because, let's face it, being human is a perpetual state of uncertainty. We never know what will happen in the next moment. We find ourselves encountering situations we did not expect despite thorough research and preparation.

There are many reasons why we may have developed a deep fear of uncertainty, and it is an uncomfortable feeling. If we allow this discomfort to be fully experienced, we notice that it is fleeting; it ebbs and flows. Yet our habit is to turn the fear and discomfort into a fixed entity and make it a problem.

We may have learned to solve this "problem" of uncertainty by becoming controlling. When we allow ourselves to be with our meditation and cultivate clear awareness of what it is that we are doing, we are given the opportunity to see how this problem-solving mode of operation shows up. We become able to recognize our pervasive fear of uncertainty without judging ourselves. Simply recognizing that the fear is part of the present moment and that we have developed a habit of turning things into a problem and activating problem-solving mode weakens the habit's hold on us.

When we relax into and stay with each emerging present moment as it unfolds, we can better notice how the mode of operation shows up in our daily life. For example, I recently encountered someone who is so attached to being a problem-solver that he turns everything into a problem. He and his family are moving into a new home, and their longtime live-in domestic helper will be leaving them at the same time. It is understandable that they would become a little stressed with two momentous changes occurring simultaneously even though the domestic helper's departure had been planned. Their child is a teenager now and can learn to look after himself, so the changes are quite manageable. And change is part of life; it is really not a problem. Nevertheless, this person who is used to planning everything thoroughly turned the situation into a problem because the uncertainty of how his family would feel about the new situation was too uncomfortable for him to bear. His solution to the "problem" was to plan every aspect of the transition thoroughly, including how his wife and son should behave and feel every step of the way. He did not want anything to deviate from his plan. He got frustrated that no one saw or addressed the "problem" he was working so hard to manage. He became stressed and agitated. Because of his agitated mind, he picked fights with his wife and child to the point that his son did not really want to be with him at all.

This is an example of how the problem-solving mode of operation is not in accordance with wisdom and compassion. By allowing an inappropriate mode of operation to be activated in such a situation, we cause ourselves unnecessary stress, tension, and suffering, and in the process contribute to the suffering of people around us. When we recognize that we have fallen into this mode of operation, we can stop perpetuating this unhelpful habit. Every moment we remember to do so, we free ourselves from unnecessary stress and suffering.

We can be so habituated to this mode that we turn not being in control into a "problem" that needs to be solved. If you have developed the belief that you are supposed to be the one in control, then noticing that things are happening without your influence is threatening. This is slightly different from the fear of uncertainty. With this belief, the body breathing on its own or a child's natural development is seen as a "problem" that cannot continue. And how do we solve this "problem"? We insert the self! We put the self in the center of the situation so that we can try to take control.

We can call this aspect of problem-solving mode "I-am-the-center-of-the-universe syndrome." What this means is that you are so attached to being the hub of each situation—the focus of attention or the person in charge of everything in every circumstance—that it is incredibly difficult to accept that other people can live their lives without your involvement. It is difficult to accept that a situation can unfold smoothly without you directing every aspect because you believe you are the person who must prevent and solve all the problems.

This reminds me of a cartoon I watched with my nephew where a rooster woke up every day at dawn and made the other chickens in the barnyard cock-a-doodle-do as loudly as they could. When the rooster was asked why they had to do this, he said their noise made the sun come up, and so they must repeat their cock-a-doodle-do every morning without fail. As the story progressed and the rooster lost his voice, he was shocked to see that the sun came up even when he was silent.

It is not uncommon to think we are the reason important events occur, people feel a certain way, or experiences unfold as they do. It is a form of self-centered attachment. One way to see this in oneself is to notice the belief that you have to control the breath in meditation. But you can also see this in many aspects of your daily life. Allow yourself to fully experience what is underlying your urge to control and then apply this understanding to your life. You may notice that underneath this urge is a fear of losing control or not being in control, or perhaps a fear of no longer being the most important person in someone's life or not being indispensable. This type of urge to control is particularly common for parents whose children are nearing adulthood. Parents are the center of a child's universe, relied upon for every aspect of survival—until they aren't. As children grow, they become increasingly self-sufficient, which is what we want to happen, yet the residual habit of being the problem-solver, the person who needs to orchestrate and take care of everything, may continue to operate. And of course, it is also possible that we enjoy playing such an essential part in someone's existence.

Regardless of what it is, this mode of operation—of thinking that not being in control is a problem—can show up in many aspects of our lives. Maybe we are training a new hire at work. In the beginning, they rely on our guidance and benefit from our experience. As they become proficient in what they are learning, they no longer need us as much. Instead of seeing that our time is now freed up to go do other things, we may become sad or even resentful to see that we are no longer essential, no longer the center of their work life.

Just as we misbelieve that it is not okay for the body to breathe on its own, we misbelieve we should be involved in things even though our involvement is unnecessary. Of course, it does not mean that we cannot be involved or engaged in a situation. The key is to understand that we are one of the causes and conditions that cocreate the situation unfolding in the present moment. It is a distorted view to see ourselves as the center of it or to believe nothing good can happen without our involvement.

Think about this in the context of a group discussion. We can be fully involved and listen attentively to the points made by others. By being fully present as we listen, we can hear both what is said and what is *not* said. Being able to feel how another person is feeling as they speak allows us to respond appropriately by contributing to the discussion constructively and letting others contribute as appropriate. In this way, we are clear that we are cocreating the situation, working with others to achieve the best possible outcome. This is quite different from operating out of the I-am-the-center-of-the-universe syndrome where we believe that we are here to drive the conversation because if we didn't nobody would have anything useful to talk about. Look to see whether this urge to turn the present moment into a problem, driven either by the fear of uncertainty or the need to be in control, shows up in your life. As we realize how doing so causes suffering for ourselves and hurts others, we are motivated to unlearn these unhelpful habits by maintaining moment-to-moment total clear awareness of our thoughts and feelings.

PERFECTIONISM

Practitioners habituated to perfectionism tend to perceive the mind drifting off the method of meditation as a major problem. To deal with the "problem," they control the breath, which is a trick many new meditators discover allows them to achieve the illusion of the perfection that they seek. When we allow ourselves to see that we are doing this in meditation, we have an opportunity to recognize what underlies the belief that control is so important—here it's an attachment to perfectionism. If you have experienced this, you will know that trying to achieve complete control in anything—meaning there is no room for any mistakes—is a tiring endeavor filled with tension. The way it shows up in meditation is that you can get frustrated every time you notice your mind has drifted off the method, although it is quite normal for the mind to be wandering. The drifting off is not a problem as long as we notice that the mind has drifted. All we need to do is to practice remembering to return to the method. That too is part of the practice. When we adhere to the idea that the perfect meditation is one in which the mind does not drift off, and we strive to achieve what we believe to be a perfect meditation record, we fill each meditation session with tension. Inevitably, what results is an agitated mind instead of a mind that is settling down, because every time the mind drifts off, we get frustrated thinking, "This is a problem" and try to fix it.

Being in problem-solving mode is a form of suffering due to our compulsion to turn the present moment into a problem, even when things are fine and there really is no problem. *The mind drifts off in meditation. It's not a problem.* It is an opportunity to practice remembering to come back to the method. And now the mind is on the method. And if the mind drifts off again, no problem. You can practice becoming more familiar with how to make use of the method, to bring your attention back and recognize that every moment is the coming together of causes and conditions and that the mind and body are not fixed entities. The reality is that they change: rhythms of breathing vary and thoughts pass through the mind. It is not a problem. But the habit of perfectionism causes us to view everything as a problem when what is happening in this present moment deviates from our ideal state of things. This deviation occurs pretty much all the time because the ideal state in our mind is an abstract idea of how things are supposed to be. It is not the fluid, constantly changing reality itself.

You may notice that perfectionism can be a major driver of problem-solving mode, especially when one is attached to being the problem-solver. Being a perfectionist means that there is always something for the problem-solver to do because at all times there is *something* that is not perfect. And since there is always a problem for the self to solve, you can see that it is quite difficult to truly relax into each emerging present moment, to allow the present moment to be as it is, to stay with this just as this. I would invite you to see if you recognize this mode of operation showing up in your meditation *and* in your daily life.

SILENCING OURSELVES

Some meditation practitioners hold the erroneous view that they are supposed to make their mind blank and solve the "problem" of thoughts by using the method to silence their thoughts. They start by identifying thoughts and feelings that arise in the mind—maybe memories, fragments of a past conversation, or images from a show they watched recently—as problems. This is related to the misbelief that what we are doing in meditation is achieving a mind with no thoughts, with nothing going on. Such a misbelief is often rooted in an incorrect understanding of concepts such as no-thought and Silent Illumination. When we believe that a mind with no thought whatsoever is the goal, then anything that shows up in the mind becomes a problem even though it is natural for thoughts to arise. There are sensory experiences, and there are activities of perception and interpretation of these sensory experiences. It is natural for there to be activities in the mind that we experience as thoughts. Sometimes particular sensations remind us of something that happened in the past and those thoughts show up. It is a natural part of being human.

Because we mistakenly believe that we should eradicate thought from our minds, we turn these thoughts into problems to be solved. One of the ways to solve the "problem" of thoughts arising in the mind is to drown out the thoughts. Practitioners who count the breath to settle the mind might repeat the number loudly in their mind and use the sound of the counting to drown out the other thoughts. This approach is usually related to controlling the breath. While controlling the breath, the practitioner would exaggerate the sensations of breath to drown out all awareness of feelings or thoughts. Often these practitioners report feeling quite calm because all they allow themselves to be aware of is the sound of counting the breath or the sensations of the breath. And more often than not, these practitioners may breathe quite loudly (sometimes disturbing others if they are in a group) because they want to strengthen the breathing sensations in the nostrils as a way to drown out their thoughts.

These problem-solving strategies for entering a state of calmness are really ways of using meditation to drown out thoughts and feelings. This especially applies to feelings of anxiety. Because we do not like the fact that we are anxious about things—an upcoming meeting, a troubled relationship, a diagnosis—we try to drown out our anxious thoughts using the method of meditation, such as following or counting the breath. Sometimes we find it helpful to take a deep breath to calm down; doing so allows us to fully reconnect with the emerging present moment and to see the situation clearly amid the anxiety. There is a subtle difference. Are we taking a breath to pause and cultivate clarity, or are we using the breath to try to block out thoughts and feelings as a way to avoid them? If it is the latter, we are adding to our suffering. What we are doing is desperately masking and blocking out feelings that are bothering us. Instead of being at ease, we are working hard to hide from thoughts and feelings that we do not want. If instead, we allow these thoughts and feelings to *be*, we will notice that what we call anxiety comes and goes; it is not fixed and it is not the problem we assume it to be. When we stay with the experience of anxiety moment to moment without trying to get rid of it and agitating the mind further in the process, we are also afforded an opportunity to see clearly where the anxiety came from and to realize that we don't have to be beholden to it.

For example, we may realize that we have done something to hurt a person in the past or broken a promise and not owned up to it. As a result, we may feel guilty or ashamed or regretful about it, and the feeling of anxiety we encounter when we meditate actually carries this information *if* we allow ourselves to truly see what is right here in the present moment. But instead of recognizing these feelings, we tend to hide from them. You may think, "These are uncomfortable feelings, so why would I want to experience and acknowledge them?" This is a fair question. Often, we believe that acknowledging these feelings can send us down a path of being ashamed and thinking we are a terrible person and further lead to beating ourselves up or self-disparagement. That is not what I am talking about here.

When we allow ourselves to recognize that we are feeling badly about what we have done, we have an opportunity to take responsibility for our actions. As soon as we acknowledge our responsibility, we may realize that the situation can be resolved quite easily. For instance, you may realize that you forgot to do something you promised you would do for a friend; thus you are worried that your friend is mad, and it is making you anxious about your upcoming meeting with them. You might realize that you are feeling guilty because you deliberately did not keep your promise when it was not convenient. By owning up to the entire situation, without blocking out any unpleasant aspects, you can take responsibility and identify an appropriate course of action. Perhaps an apology is due. Maybe there is still time for you to keep your promise. Maybe you can find out what you can do to make up for the mistake. Whatever it is, by acknowledging instead of obscuring, you can prevent the situation from getting worse.

This is related to the habit of perfectionism that leaves no room for mistakes. As humans, we all make mistakes. It is not a problem. Recognizing that we have made a mistake and learning from it is how we grow. It does not mean that a relationship is permanently damaged. By being willing to acknowledge your mistake and that you may have hurt someone, you can repair and even deepen the relationship. When you allow these thoughts and feelings to be fully experienced rather than busying yourself with silencing and blocking them out, whether through improper approaches to meditation or by trying to control aspects of your life too tightly, you can connect with your experience *and* with the people in your life more fully.

RETURNING TO SILENT ILLUMINATION

Every moment is the coming together of causes and conditions. Staying with each emerging present moment as it is will allow us to recognize the deep-seated fear of uncertainty within us and how it compels us to activate the problem-solving mode to mask and suppress this fear. Our resistance to the true nature of reality—every moment being brand-new and thus uncertain—shows up as fear of failure, fear of making mistakes, or fear of losing control.

In the practice of Silent Illumination, whatever happens in each moment, let through, let be, let go. The fear of and resistance to uncertainty are allowed into awareness and fully experienced as they are. When we practice this way, we realize how we have been trying to silence our fear by turning the present moment into a problem, busying ourselves with fixing and controlling reality instead of allowing ourselves to be, to stay with this just as this. In the process, we have made life much harder than it needs to be for ourselves and for others.

Very often, we meant well and wanted to be helpful with our problem-solving. Without clear awareness of this mode of operation, however, we cause suffering for ourselves and harm others. We feel hurt when others do not appreciate our help and lash out at them, creating yet more "problems" for us to solve. We can drag everyone in our life into this vicious cycle for the rest of our lives if we are not careful. Meanwhile, we are blocking ourselves from reconnecting with the true nature of our being and fully engaging with life as it unfolds in each emerging present moment. When we only see problems, we deprive ourselves of the sense of wonder and connectedness available in each moment. There may be fear but we do not need to let it control us. In fact, when fear of uncertainty arises, it reminds us of our habitual resistance to the true nature of reality and the need to practice. Instead of seeing it as a foe to suppress, we can treat it as our friend who reminds us to practice. With time, it no longer matters whether the fear of uncertainty arises or not.

This does not mean that we do not fulfill our responsibilities or handle issues when they arise. As we practice Silent Illumination, we are clear about what needs to be done by us, what is better handled with or by someone else, and what needs more time to work itself out. When we are not compulsively turning the present moment into a problem and wearing ourselves out trying to fix everything, we make good use of our time and energy by fulfilling our responsibilities wholeheartedly in the world we cocreate with others. Everyone benefits when we do our part well. That is compassion. We are not causing ourselves unnecessary suffering. That is wisdom.

10

INTELLECTUALIZING MODE
Thinking Our Way to Enlightenment

Intellectualizing mode is the entrenched habit of substituting concepts for direct experience. Practitioners operating in this mode are accustomed to reacting to the present moment by invoking a concept acquired from past experience or learning and mistaking it for the present-moment experience itself. Attaching to ideas turns the world into reified objects and causes suffering. In contrast, cultivating clear awareness of each moment as the coming together of constantly changing causes and conditions allows us to live in accordance with wisdom and compassion.

Concepts, ideas . . . we love them. We are addicted to them because they give us the illusion that we are actually experiencing what is represented by the concepts. Reading and thinking about swimming in a lake may trick us into believing that we know what it's like to swim in a lake. If we have ever tried doing something we've only read about, we realize that it's rarely like what we imagined. When we dwell on concepts and mistake them for direct experience, we are missing much of life itself.

When asked how their meditation is going, practitioners operating in this mode often say their practice is going well and that they have come to see that their thoughts are "just" wandering thoughts: "There are thoughts passing through. I know it is just emptiness and impermanence." Yet this means they are not really paying attention to them. Or they might say, "Why pay attention to thoughts? They are illusory anyway." These are telltale signs that one is engaging in the mode of intellectualizing. These practitioners are substituting Dharma concepts, such as emptiness and the illusory nature of thoughts, for direct experience of the thoughts and feelings moment to moment. They are not cultivating clarity of the activities of the mind, which is why the mode of intellectualizing renders it difficult to realize the true nature of mind.

When these practitioners hear "let through, let be, let go," they use the concept to label their present-moment experience: "Here is a wandering thought. Here is another wandering thought. This is empty. This is impermanent." While the method of noting thoughts can be helpful for stabilizing the mind, practitioners need to be careful not to inadvertently block thoughts and feelings from being fully experienced, heard, and seen moment to moment. When they use concepts like impermanence to label their experience, there can be a subtle shift in their attention away from the experience itself to the concept used to label it. This is what I mean by substituting concepts for direct experience.

For instance, thoughts, feelings, and images from a difficult memory may emerge in our mind. As soon as we label the moment with the concept like "It's just a memory," we stop paying attention to the emerging present moment. As we turn the experience into a fixed entity by reifying it as *that* memory, we assume we already know what the emerging present moment is. This habitual tendency—assuming we already know—compels us to stop paying attention to the present-moment experience of recalling this memory. Since we are convinced that we *already* know, there is no curiosity to help us maintain moment-to-moment clear awareness. We are no longer fully present and cannot experience each moment as it is—the coming together of causes and conditions.

When we perceive an experience as a fixed entity, we are prone to the habit of judging it as good or bad, in turn activating the habits of craving and aversion. The subtle thought, "It's 'just' a thought—not what I want. I want to realize emptiness. I want enlightenment" compels us to try to let go of the thought, but what we're really doing is forcing it to go away. Intellectualizing is a type of aversion as we try to push the thought out of awareness. It is the habit of feeling that whatever is happening in the present moment is not what I want and not good enough. This is suffering.

LABELS ARE NOT REALITY AS IT IS

The habit of labeling an experience with a concept also generalizes the experience. When we say to ourselves, "It's a thought. It's another thought. It's all just thoughts," we are not cultivating clarity of the nuances during the moment-to-moment experiences that are being labeled as "just thoughts." Every moment is glossed over, and there is a lack of clarity. Our attachment to the concept drives us to overlook and block out aspects of the present that do not fit neatly into the concept used to label our experience. If we label a memory as a "terrible time," moments of happiness and gratitude are not allowed into awareness as they do not fit under the label of that experience being "terrible." This blocking of certain aspects of our experience agitates the mind; it is not silence and it is not illumination.

When we fall into the habit of substituting concepts for directly experiencing each emerging present moment, we are not gaining insight into the subtle habits of the mind. We are not able to see how we are triggered into activating various modes of operation. Nor are we able to realize that every moment is truly the coming together of changing causes and conditions, which allows us to connect with the wisdom of emptiness. We can get bored with the practice, feeling a bit lost as we keep telling ourselves, "This is empty, that is impermanent." Being stuck on concepts, we fail to experience the vitality and dynamic nature of life as it really is.

We may also turn our attention to complex theories of mind to give ourselves the illusion that we are practicing the Dharma. Dharma study is indeed useful for establishing right view and developing correct understanding of important Dharma concepts such as emptiness. However, it is important to remember that a doctorate in Buddhist studies is not essential to directly experience ourselves. We just need to be here, fully present with each emerging moment. If your "solution" to the "problems" in your practice is always to read more Dharma books and seek comfort in the concepts, this mode of operation may be part of your entrenched habitual tendency to avoid aspects of yourself or your life.

There is no need to be frustrated or embarrassed. Concepts are tempting and alluring. They appear neat and tidy. Reality, however, does not fit precisely into the boxes defined by concepts. Because of that, reality feels messy. Notice your tendency to attach to that which feels neat and tidy. We can fall into the habit of trying to figure out when a phenomenon crosses a conceptual line into another category, such as whether it is sensation or perception, and fool ourselves into thinking that we are practicing. Instead of cultivating clear awareness, we go down conceptual rabbit holes while perpetuating unhelpful habitual tendencies without awareness, causing suffering for ourselves and others.

PRACTICING NOT KNOWING

Theories, including even the most profound Dharma teachings, are no substitute for directly experiencing our mind in Silent Illumination. The practice of Silent Illumination invites us to be here—just here—with this body and mind in this space as it is. Yet our minds prefer to do something that appears similar but is quite different. The dialogue in your head might be something like "I am practicing. I can view sensation that is conditioned by contact. This must be the stuff I read about in Dharma books or heard about on that famous teacher's podcast. I can feel emptiness! I am experiencing impermanence!" What we are doing here is substituting concepts, labels, and Dharma theories for direct experience.

Check to see if you like the *idea* of meditating more than the actual practice of meditation. The idea of practice feels neat and tidy, a linear process you can read about in Dharma books and hear described in podcasts: you settle the mind and experience unified mind and then no-mind. However, the reality of practice is a lot messier. You may settle your mind a little bit, but then the thoughts you have been working hard to suppress pop up whether you want them to or not, leading to agitation because you didn't want these thoughts and tried to block them out. Then you remember that there is no need to suppress thoughts; you relax into each emerging present moment, and the mind settles. Before you know it, a craving for the mind to be calmer arises, tensing up the mind until you remember to release the compulsion to crave, and the mind settles. This is how the process of settling the mind in meditation practice goes in reality.

Notice if reading this makes you feel uncomfortable or unhappy because these words are not meeting your expectation of how your practice is supposed to be! We like to use concepts to give us the comfort that we already know how our practice will progress, when in fact we should give up all of our preconceived notions and allow the freshness and newness of each moment to emerge. We can do this by remembering that every single moment is the coming together of many causes and conditions. This is how we cultivate right view.

In Chan, there is a teaching called the "mind of not knowing." Some people misunderstand this expression, believing it means not using the mind to think, and thus they consider Chan practice to be about not thinking. That is not what the teaching is about, nor what Silent Illumination is about, and it is not what the Buddha taught. The mind of not knowing doesn't mean *not* being discerning, nor does it mean *not* using our analytical capacity to consider the information we receive to make sound judgments and respond appropriately to situations we encounter in life. What it means is letting go of the unhelpful habit of believing we already know what is still unfolding in the present moment, and what is going to unfold in the next moment. Remember, every moment is the coming together of causes and conditions and is brand-new. This moment has never happened before. We may have experienced similar ones, but we are now a different person, and the exact current conditions are unique. It is an erroneous view to believe we already know this emerging moment. This belief represents our attachment to conceptual thoughts, and it blocks us from paying close attention and being fully, clearly aware of what is emerging in the present.

HOW INTELLECTUALIZING GETS IN THE WAY OF PRACTICE

Many people engage in intellectualizing because they are intellectuals. They are enamored with ideas and love words and concepts more than the direct experience of themselves and the world. Often, these individuals prefer ideas because they are safe—defined and compartmentalized, neat and tidy—compared to the messiness of what we call "reality." I have met many people who are really good at intellectualizing. Usually they are well-read, they've studied lots of Dharma books or analyzed heavy-duty sutras or sophisticated Zen discourses, and they may even have advanced degrees in Buddhist studies. They have a great interest in analyzing the meditative experience to label it with concepts, and in talking and thinking about things rather than allowing themselves to experience their mind as it is moment after moment.

Conceptual analysis can only capture fragments of the continuous flow of experience, highlighting certain moments while downplaying others. When the mind is settled and clear, we may be able to observe the ins and outs of our subtle meditative experiences and describe and analyze them in great detail. Such analysis can be useful for understanding Dharma concepts, but we need to remember that the conceptual analysis is not the experience itself. Conceptualizing the state of Silent Illumination is not the practice of Silent Illumination. The conceptualizing gets in the way of direct experience.

Practitioners who forget that concepts are abstract representations of experience and not the experience itself become habituated to the intellectualizing mode and can even form an idealized notion about the practice. Operating in this mode, for instance, when we encounter the word *stillness* in the teachings of Silent Illumination, we imagine a state of perfect stillness that is not grounded in the actual experience of stillness. We hold this idea of stillness in mind as the ideal with which we judge each moment of our meditation. The idea of stillness implies an opposition to nonstillness; everything that does not fit into our imagined ideal of stillness falls under "nonstillness" and is judged as a failure. Since our idea of stillness is imagined, we will inevitably find our present-moment experience falling short, generating unsatisfactoriness. This is suffering. Instead of staying with this just as this, we hold on to the concept to feel in control.

Very often, when something comes up in our meditation practice, we immediately draw on concepts we've learned in an effort to understand it, hoping that we can break through obstacles in our mind through conceptual understanding. For instance, some practitioners might try to figure out whether a thought is a sensation, perception, or volition, hoping that it will help them discover where clinging occurs so that they know when to let go. They are, in fact, substituting language for the direct experience of what is unfolding in the moment and end up getting stuck in the concepts.

Direct experience defies conceptual thinking. Concepts are useful to highlight aspects of reality that enable us to analyze and communicate our experience. Conceptual understanding is, however, no substitute for the depth and clarity of knowing that arises from direct experience. Master Sheng Yen liked to use the analogy of knowing what water is. We can conduct exhaustive research on all existing descriptions of water, yet it remains an abstract concept. No matter what we imagine water to be like based on these descriptions, it is not that. Reading more descriptions of water will not bring us closer to knowing how water tastes and feels. All we need to do is to take a sip of water, and then we know. Dharma teachings are like descriptions of water by those who have tasted water. Holding on to other people's words derived from *their* experience is like counting other people's treasures; they will not become ours.

Concepts are seductive. They give us the illusion of achieving what is being represented. Master Sheng Yen liked to talk about this habit by using the analogy of studying the menu instead of eating the food. We go to a restaurant to eat because we are hungry. Similarly, we come to the practice because we suffer and would like to find a way to end suffering. The description of food on the menu is based on someone else's experience of eating the food. We can fantasize about how tasty the food will be by reading the menu, but if we try to satisfy our appetite without actually eating any food, we will still be hungry. Similarly, if we mistake reading Dharma books for practicing, for directly experiencing each moment as it is, we will be like the hungry person who reads a menu without eating. We will continue to generate suffering for ourselves and others.

When we experience ourselves directly, instead of indirectly through our ideas of ourselves and reality, we realize that which is inconceivable—that is, an experience that cannot be fully conveyed in words and ultimately must be experienced to be truly understood. This is what is meant by the Chan teaching of "not relying on words." Our strong attachment to concepts leads us to mistake words, concepts, ideas, and descriptions for reality itself, blocking us from the wondrous present moment that is with us all the time *right now*. Are you fully here to experience it?

DISCOMFORT AND FEAR OF EMPTINESS

We do not need to be intellectuals to engage in the habit of intellectualizing. For people who fall into intellectualizing mode, when something comes up in their meditation, they instantly label the experience with words and tell themselves that they already know what is happening. The thought "I already know" basically tells us we can stop paying attention. We dull our awareness of the moment-to-moment experience, falling out of the practice. This is a way of using concepts to control reality because allowing reality to unfold seems too scary for some.

Nobody wants to be afraid, so you might secretly wish, "If I understand these Dharma concepts well enough, maybe I can make reality fit into them." You can see why that requires a lot of unnecessary effort and creates tension instead of clear awareness. It is a strategy for constructing a sense that we already know what is going to happen instead of dealing with the discomfort of not knowing what is going to emerge in the next moment. The root of this discomfort is our aversion to a reality of life—uncertainty—where every moment is a coming together of changing causes and conditions. In this sometimes-subtle level of intellectualizing, thoughts allow us to maintain distance and avoid directly experiencing what is happening in the mind. It is not "letting be" because these subtle motions of mind block and restrict our experience of the natural flow of the present moment. This is not Silent Illumination.

Often, intellectualizing is about more than just discomfort; it also has to do with our fear. We might be afraid of what we'll discover or experience if we allow ourselves to see into our mind directly. Because of this fear, we invoke a concept to describe the experience and thereby trick ourselves into thinking we already understand. All we've done is apply a label instead of allowing our mind to rest where it is and truly paying attention. Perhaps we are afraid of what we might discover, so we outsmart ourselves right back into a place of suffering.

We not only trick ourselves into thinking we already know those experiences that cause discomfort or fear, but our habitual reaction to the fear itself can also cause suffering. When we label an emotion "fear," the habit of assuming we already know this particular fear is activated. We stop paying attention and are no longer really allowing the present moment to be fully experienced, heard, and seen. Because we are afraid of this "fear," we are ready to "let it go," meaning we are in a hurry to push it out of our awareness. Our mind tenses up and is agitated; it is suffering. In the practice of Silent Illumination, when we allow what underlies the label of "fear" to be fully experienced moment to moment, we may notice it is not all fear. We may find excitement, hope, happiness, anticipation, or anxiety all mixed together. By looking away from our fear we fail to see its true nature and our complex relationships to it.

We might also notice that we conceptualize our fear in order to fit it into our preferred narrative of what is happening. If we allow each emerging present moment to be fully experienced, we gain insight into our true self. We can see how we are controlled by our narratives about ourselves and the world—narratives we created at some point in the past—and that these narratives are not the entirety of our reality. When we recognize this, we can free ourselves from our narratives and see ourselves, our lives, and the present moment as if for the first time.

As we look beyond the labels, we gain insight into how our habit of reifying our experiences and turning them into monolithic, solid entities compels us to become disconnected from the present moment. We can see for ourselves how the intellectualizing mode gets in the way of our connection with reality as it is, our self as it is. We can let go of the habit of holding on to an idea as a substitute for direct experience and relax into each emerging present moment.

Check to see if you operate in this mode out of discomfort or fear and because you are assuming that, when you look into your mind, whatever you find is not going to be that great. To preempt the unpleasant experience, do you block it out of your awareness? Do you think you already know what your next experience is going to be? Perhaps you haven't really looked. You may find something wonderful about yourself—a great capacity to be loving, to be generous, to be kind. But you can't see it if you obscure it with assumptions about who you are.

Some people also adopt the intellectualizing mode of operation in their meditation practice due to a very specific fear—the fear of emptiness. This is because they have an incorrect understanding of the concept. They believe emptiness means nonexistence or nothingness. They may have read or been told that the mind or the self is "empty," and they fear seeing their own nonexistence, which *again* is an incorrect understanding of the teaching of emptiness. The teaching of emptiness points to the fact that every moment is the coming together of constantly changing causes and conditions; everything exists but not as inherently existing entities with fixed characteristics. If instead these practitioners allow themselves to fully experience the present moment, they will realize their preconceived idea of the present moment—the self, the situation—does not capture the richness of everything that is happening.

As we explore the mode of intellectualizing it becomes increasingly clear that words can get in our way. The moment we begin to conceptualize, we are no longer staying with this just as this. When we allow the present moment to be fully experienced, instead of blocking it with concepts and words, we can connect with the richness and fullness of the moment. When we do, we will truly put our fears to rest.

LIMITING OUR CAPACITY FOR COMPASSION

When we conceptualize and intellectualize and avoid the messiness of life, we are avoiding the truth of who we are and of the here and now. Intellectualizing practitioners who are not actually cultivating clear awareness in their meditation may find the same thing occurring in their daily lives. They are disconnected from their environment, the people around them, and parts of themselves.

One way the intellectualizing mode shows up in everyday life is through the habit of labeling a situation to insulate ourselves from the unpleasant aspects of that situation, while believing that we are being a good practitioner. For instance, when we encounter the news that a loved one is dying, we might invoke the Dharma concept of impermanence to label what is happening and disengage from our grief. We stop being fully present with all the thoughts and feelings that arise upon receiving difficult news. We do not allow ourselves to process the sadness, love, pain, fear, and myriad other thoughts—some less coherent than others—and instead use concepts to block out these thoughts and feelings.

Without clarity, we are prone to fall into unhelpful habits that cause suffering for ourselves and others. If we are not in touch with how we feel then we are also not in touch with how others feel and what their needs are. We are then unable to discern the appropriate action to take. We may find it difficult to connect with a suffering or dying person because we are hiding behind the concept of impermanence or death instead of fully engaging with the unfolding situation. As we disconnect and create distance from our sadness, we may even tell others that they should not be sad and should understand that this is impermanence!

While it is true that life is impermanent, what we are doing is activating the intellectualizing mode to disengage from the actual *experience* of impermanence in the present moment. We may think we sound wise by invoking a Dharma concept, but we are depriving ourselves (and sometimes others) of the opportunity for growth by fully experiencing the process of a loved one leaving us. As painful as it may be, maintaining clear awareness of the moment-to-moment experience of any situation, alone or with others, ultimately allows us to be at peace. Allowing ourselves to experience all of our thoughts and feelings enables us to empathize with those who have lost their loved ones. Instead of strengthening our capacity for compassion, operating in intellectualizing mode restricts our capacity to be compassionate. Our urge to disengage from and avoid the situation by invoking concepts leaves both ourselves and others feeling unsupported and unloved.

INTELLECTUALIZING AS A MEANS TO DISENGAGE AND DISCONNECT

We may also activate the intellectualizing mode to avoid dealing with the messy reality of life. When there is conflict and disagreement in a group, we may invoke Dharma concepts such as vexation to explain things away, telling ourselves that we already know what is happening. This gives us permission to stop listening and start disengaging. We want to stay above the fray and not get involved in the "mess." We don't want to let the situation disturb our peace. By doing this, we are not fulfilling our responsibility of being a member of the group, especially when others look to us for guidance, friendship, or leadership. By listening and paying attention to everyone's reasoning and the group's dynamic, we can contribute to the resolution of the situation. It may be in the form of de-escalating conflict by making people feel heard, or we may be able to identify a way forward that addresses the grievance. At the very least, we can avoid contributing to the suffering of everyone involved by not using the approach of labeling the situation with a concept to disengage and block what is happening out of our awareness. When we label, disengage, and block, this is not silence and there is no clarity.

Another way this mode shows up in life is when we mistake what we read or hear about a place or a group for the *reality* of the place or the group. When we encounter an individual from the group, we might assume that we already know who they are. Because of this we tend to not listen to and see this person as they are in the present moment. Instead, we rely on our preconceived notion and use it as a point of reference to judge this person, often concluding that something is not quite right. We lack the clarity to see that we feel this way because we are not fully present with this person and allowing ourselves to connect as fellow human beings. Not being seen as who we are is painful. Refusing to see someone for who they are is not in accordance with wisdom and compassion.

Intellectualizing is not just a mode favored by new meditators. Some people may practice for many years and be fluent in Dharma concepts and theories and able to use them to analyze subtle things that happen in their mind, but they have no awareness of what is going on in the world or with the people around them. They live in their imagined world of neatly labeled and boxed concepts and ideas. They may be hiding from the messy parts of life—unresolved or seemingly unresolvable situations and relationships, financial troubles, or health or family difficulties.

Similarly, some people like the idea of being part of a community for the sense of belonging and support it can provide, yet they avoid the reality of fully engaging in the practice with others as that could also involve disagreement, conflict, and disappointment. That is *not* direct experience of community. The same applies to people who like the idea of practicing Chan.

Check to see if you do this because of a preference for or attachment to ideas and concepts as a substitute for direct experience. We all have this strong tendency to prefer the idea of doing something over the actual doing of something. And it can be such an entrenched habit that we are not even aware of it. We fool ourselves into believing that the idea of doing something is the act of doing of it. Sometimes we can't even tell the difference. It's like watching videos of exercising instead of exercising or making lists of tasks you're going to complete instead of doing them.

RETURNING TO SILENT ILLUMINATION

Let's return to Master Sheng Yen's analogy about food. There are people who say they love cooking. They spend a lot of time watching cooking shows or reading cookbooks, but they do not make dinner! They do not actually cook. They do not roll up their sleeves and get their hands and the kitchen dirty. Watching cooking shows is quite a different experience. We do not need to get hot and sweaty over the stove, try new recipes and sometimes fail, and of course, wash the dishes afterward. Somehow in our mind, we believe we're doing a lot of cooking. Yet, when we are hungry, we often get up from the cooking show and order takeout or warm up a frozen dinner. Check to see if you do something similar to this when it comes to practice.

The habit of intellectualizing can cause quite a serious lack of clarity and a lot of suffering. When we do not recognize that we operate in this mode, we expend energy going into Dharma books, trying to gain realization by probing the meaning of the words, and mistaking this for the practice. We believe that the practice is about getting the words right. We may become so engrossed with the ideas of silence and illumination that we miss the entire point—actually stilling and illuminating our own mind. Hence, we may be working very hard in what we believe to be the practice, yet we are not looking into the moment-to-moment mind.

Without clarity of our habitual tendencies, we continue to act them out and cause suffering to ourselves and others. This is not in accordance with wisdom and compassion. When we feel the urge to focus on the Dharma concepts as a substitute for direct experience, it is helpful to remember that these concepts are like a finger pointing at the moon. Its function is to direct us to the path, to encourage us to reconnect with the reality of the self as it is by looking into the mind. If we study the finger and ignore the moon altogether, we are operating in the intellectualizing mode. It is unfortunate. Remember, Dharma is the finger pointing to the moon, guiding us to directly experience ourselves as we are. If we try to look for the answer in words, we are causing more of our own suffering by trying to fit our experience into these concepts.

In the practice of Silent Illumination, we cultivate clear awareness of the subtle actions of our mind moment to moment. In so doing, we become familiar with the triggers that activate intellectualizing mode and how the chain of thoughts and feelings that constitute the habit—labeling, believing that we already know and no longer need to pay attention, disconnecting from direct experience, getting stuck in concepts—unfolds once the mode is activated. As the chain is activated and progresses, we can choose not to give rise to the next thought in the sequence. With this clarity, we can notice the subtle shifts that disconnect us from our direct experience and how we substitute it with words and concepts. We can reconnect fully with the direct experience of the present moment. As we unlearn the entrenched habit of reacting to the present moment by intellectualizing, we fully engage with life as it is moment after moment, opening our heart to embrace everything in Silent Illumination.

11

QUIETISM MODE
Dwelling in a Dark Cave

Quietism is suffering created by attachment to a state of nothingness that we mistake for the realization of emptiness. It
is the misguided habit of abiding in "silence" as an absence
of thoughts and at the expense of illumination. Underlying
quietism is an aversion to that which is perceived to be defiled
or worldly. It is based on an erroneous view that nirvana is
separate from and in opposition to samsara, that enlightenment is separate from life. Careful examination of one's views
and the cultivation of right view are crucial for releasing our
attachment to quietism.

Think about how quietism occurs when we practice. After
sitting in meditation for an extended period where we iso-
late ourselves from our daily affairs, we may find ourselves in
a peaceful state. In this state, the mind becomes very quiet;
there is hardly any thought. The difference can be quite stark if
we are used to an active mind with lots of planning, analyzing,

and arguing. When we practice in a silent retreat where we drastically reduce mental stimuli by refraining from social interactions and receiving news from the outside world via email or phone messages, it is normal for the mind to quiet down. In other words, the quiet state of mind is conditioned by isolating ourselves from the world. We get into trouble when we mistake this quiet state of mind for the ultimate state, believing that it is the destination to abide in. With this erroneous view, we may believe that we have achieved "silence" and thus become unwilling to give it up by opening our awareness to stay with thoughts and feelings just as thoughts and feelings.

Because we are convinced that this quiet state is the right one and an indication of good practice, we tend to experience resistance upon hearing the instruction to "let through, let be, let go." I have met practitioners who were stuck in quietism and resisted vehemently when instructed to open their awareness to thoughts and feelings. They couldn't believe they were being told to let thoughts through after they worked so hard to block out thoughts in their effort to stay with the method. No matter how many times the instruction to "let through, let be, let go" is given, these practitioners cling to the quietude and are convinced that they are being misled. Some might tell me they tried opening their awareness and found the mind gets too noisy, so they shut that down right away. Some would refuse to acknowledge that they were resisting opening their awareness. These are signs that a meditator is attached to quietism, clinging to a false idea of stillness with the conviction that the quiet mind is what is right, implying that its opposite—noise—is bad and should be avoided. Noticing this strong resistance will help you release this unhelpful habit.

When we apply a method, such as counting or following the breath, to settle the mind, it is important to take care not to train the mind to be reactive but instead maintain clear awareness of each emerging present moment. As the mind settles and becomes less agitated and confused, we can see subtle thoughts and feelings more clearly and gain insight into our habitual tendencies. This allows us to see thoughts for what they are, to see our entrenched habits for what they are—a chain of thoughts and habits that we do not need to keep perpetuating. This is how we can unlearn the habit of reacting with vexations and stop generating suffering.

Practicing this way, we can see that a quiet mind is the coming together of causes and conditions and is impermanent. When causes and conditions change—perhaps when we engage in social interactions—thoughts and feelings will show up. It's not a problem. For practitioners habituated to quietism, however, the quiet state is considered the right state of mind to abide in, and "noise" from opening our awareness should be avoided. This means there is no clear awareness of the subtle and entrenched habits of the mind that generate suffering. The mind may be quiet, yet without clarity of how these habits operate, we will continue to react with our habits and cause harm when we interact with others in the world. If we mistake quietism for good practice, we are depriving ourselves of the opportunity to free ourselves from the habit of suffering.

QUIETISM IS NOT SILENT ILLUMINATION

Incorrect understanding of the practice of Silent Illumination can trap us in quietism. Master Dahui was particularly critical of what he called "perverted Silent Illumination," which considers wordlessness or the absence of thought as the ultimate principle.[14] He was referring to the tendency to associate "silence" with the lack of mental activities. This kind of silence is like the absence of ripples on a pond inside a vacuum. There is no moving air that touches the water surface, nor are there leaves falling or insects alighting on the pond. The pond is quiet. It is also lifeless.

In Silent Illumination, we are fully engaged in life. There is clarity of everything including thoughts and feelings in the present moment while our entrenched habit of reacting with vexations is not activated. This nonreactivity is the "silence" in Silent Illumination. We can experience powerful emotions such as sadness upon learning about the death of a loved one; they can be fully allowed, processed, and released without activating the habit of resistance. Without our habitual reactivity, there is no hatred toward what is happening nor wishing it would be otherwise. Nonetheless, we are fully present with the sadness while allowing everything else—be it gratitude, anger, relief, or regret—to be acknowledged, experienced, and released. We fully experience our thoughts and emotions moment after moment without being emotional. Thoughts and emotions are fully embraced as part of each emerging present moment, not noise to be avoided so that we may abide in quietude.

If we practice with the erroneous view that Silent Illumination is about dwelling in quietude, we train ourselves to dismiss thoughts and feelings. We do this by closing our hearts so as not to be disturbed. We avoid feeling painful emotions. When we do this, we also miss out on feeling joy and connection. Detached from our pain and anxiety, we cannot empathize with those who are struggling. There is no illumination whatsoever. We are barely alive!

This reminds me of the story of a monk in ancient China who engaged in solitary practice with the support of an elderly woman who brought him food. After supporting this monk for a long time, the old woman sent her daughter, an attractive young woman, in her place. The young woman embraced the monk. The next time she visited, the old woman asked the monk, "How did you feel when my daughter embraced you?" The monk replied, "Like cold ashes and a dry log." The old woman chased him out of his hermitage. It was clear to her that this monk was cultivating an erroneous view, believing that the practice was about turning himself into an unfeeling person.

When we make the mistake of emphasizing and dwelling in quietude at the expense of illumination, we may be able to sit in stillness, but we are not practicing. As you may recall, Master Sheng Yen called it soaking a stone in cold water. What happens when we do this? Nothing. We are not cultivating clarity of how our habitual reactivity shows up and we are not unlearning these habits by allowing them to be fully experienced. We may be able to sit in meditation session after session in long retreats, but we are not practicing.

As Master Sheng Yen would say, "You are not practicing. You are resting." We are taking a break from reality, hiding from the stress and difficulty in life. But this is not Silent Illumination. We need to be clear about this. We are fooling ourselves by going through the motion of sitting in meditation if we are not investigating the mind to look into our entrenched habits of vexation. We are not cultivating wisdom if we are not seeing that each emerging moment truly is the coming together of causes and conditions. If we are fixated on a blank nothingness, we waste our precious opportunity to gain insight into our mind and to be fully connected with ourselves. Not only do we allow the habit of suffering to continue, but we are emotionally unavailable to bring joy and happiness to others.

BEWARE THE ROAD TO THE DARK CAVE

John Crook often said, "Chan is not supposed to be comfortable." If you notice you are just resting in quietude, cultivate clear awareness of what it is that you are hiding from. How are you, thought after thought, constructing a dark cave in which to sit and hide from the world and from yourself? We may believe there is no thought when in fact we lack clarity to see how we are operating to block awareness. Stay with each emerging present moment as you experience resistance to opening your awareness and letting light into the dark cave.

We may believe that we have found safety in this dark cave, therefore we need to fully experience this yearning for absolute safety and a permanent abode to gain insight into our vexations. As my current teacher Simon Child likes to say in retreats, "As we sit in this dark cave believing we are safe, we have no idea that there is a sleeping bear behind us that is about to wake up." It is not the sanctuary we may assume. When we realize that we are deluded, Master Dahui urged, wake up! To remain deluded would be doubly deluded. When we realize that we are attached to quietism, we need to pay attention and allow thoughts into awareness even if that means having a busy mind. When we know our mind this way, the way it really is, we can cultivate clarity about how it works. Otherwise, our entrenched habits and erroneous views fester in darkness and, like the sleeping bear, can sneak up on us as we sit in oblivion.

Don't assume you are not prone to fall into quietism, that you won't enter that dark cave. We may think our mind is usually scattered and busy and that we are just trying to settle down the mind, that being stuck in quietism seems like a distant possibility. But in many of his letters to students, Master Dahui warned that it is not uncommon for practitioners to end up in quietism. Similarly, Master Sheng Yen repeatedly warned us against dwelling in the dark cave during a forty-nine-day Silent Illumination retreat attended by many of his most serious and long-term students. It is important to pay attention to how we are approaching the practice so that we are not inadvertently taking up residence in the dark cave.

When you encounter Dharma teachings and practice instructions, pay close attention not only to the teachings but also to your reactions to them. In meditation practice using the method of breath to settle the mind, for instance, how do you view thoughts? Do you interpret descriptions of thoughts being "illusory" as meaning they are bad and you should dismiss them because you are trying to realize the ultimate? Do you consider wandering thoughts "defilements" of the "pure mind" you want to achieve? When you encounter Dharma teachings such as "beyond words," "forgetting all words," or "no thought," do you interpret them to mean that thoughts are obstructions from which you need to free yourself?

Pay attention to the subtle habits of interpreting and judging that compel us to react in ways that privilege quietude at the expense of awareness. If we believe illusory thoughts are not part of the ultimate that we strive to realize, we will be habituated to dismiss them. We will not understand the importance of allowing them to be fully experienced, heard, and seen, and we will resist the instruction to "let through, let be, and let go" in Silent Illumination. If we believe we are here to achieve a "pure mind" that is not "defiled" by thoughts, we will keep thoughts and feelings out of awareness, perhaps by hiding in a cave to protect the mind from being defiled. If we believe words and thoughts are obstructions, we will work to clear those obstructions by closing our awareness and avoiding stimuli, as we vehemently protect the quiet mind from invasion by thoughts. Instructions to open our awareness will feel like threats that trigger fight-or-flight responses. Notice these subtle reactions and reflect on your interpretation of Dharma teachings so that you do not unknowingly slip onto the path toward quietism. Remind yourself that "going beyond words" and "forgetting all words" do not mean dismissing words. Silent Illumination does not mean clearing your mind of thoughts.

We are all prone to these erroneous understandings due to the entrenched habit of dualistic thinking. For example, we may believe there are Dharma practice activities that are in opposition to non-Dharma-practice activities. Or we may associate the practice with what is transcendent and sacred in opposition to nonpractice activities that we regard as worldly and profane. We may believe samsara (the cycle of suffering) is separate from and in opposition to nirvana (the cessation of suffering). We view quietude in opposition to commotion. Concepts are tools to highlight and communicate aspects of reality, but each concept implies its opposite—they are dualistic by nature. When we reify these concepts, we reify dualism. Some of us are habituated to turn the conceptual opposites into good and evil in absolute terms. This is not Silent Illumination.

If we have the tendency to perceive the world in this way, we will see nirvana as absolutely good and a separate samsara as absolutely bad. We will see Master Huineng's teaching of "samsara is nirvana" and "vexation is *prajna*" (or wisdom), meant to help free us from dualistic thinking, as incomprehensible. In a similar manner, we may mistakenly draw a clear line separating what is practice and what is nonpractice—between what is transcendent and what is worldly—and view the former as absolutely good and the latter as absolutely bad. The Chan teaching "Ordinary mind is the way" is meant to help untangle us from these extreme views. If we believe practice is about clearing thoughts from the mind and that thoughts and feelings are worldly and bad, we will cling to quietude as an absolute good and detest commotion. We will fortify our dark cave to protect ourselves from worldly thoughts.

The cultivation of clear awareness of our moment-to-moment experience is crucial in recognizing our tendency to turn Dharma concepts into absolute opposites, attaching to one extreme while vehemently rejecting the other. When we allow these extreme views to be fully experienced, we will notice how powerfully they drive our actions and run our lives, leaving wreckage in their wake. This realization will help us muster the courage to open our awareness and release these extreme views. We will see that allowing thoughts and feelings into our mind is not blasphemy. It is staying with this just as this, the practice of Silent Illumination. As we work with ourselves skillfully and patiently, we can free ourselves from the dark cave constructed by our strong attachment to extreme views and come to appreciate our interconnectedness.

QUIETISM IN OUR LIVES

Our attachment to quietism in meditation often shows up in how we live. These ways of living are not problematic in and of themselves. They are often considered healthy lifestyles. What we need to pay attention to is how we relate to them. Do we believe that ours is absolutely the right way to live? Are we judgmental of others who live differently? For instance, our attachment to quietude may lead us to keep our life simple. We may stick to the same routine every day, perhaps in solitude whenever possible. We stay away from gatherings and avoid getting involved in complicated situations. This is a fine lifestyle, however, check to see if you stay away from social gatherings because they are "too noisy" and avoid situations involving other people because they are "too complicated." The frequent use of "too" is an indication of a judgmental attitude toward activities we believe we should avoid. Be attentive and listen to your speech and thoughts to see if you are building a wall to separate yourself from the world.

Our attachment to discriminating between practice and nonpractice—between the transcendent and the worldly—compels us to dwell in activities associated with practice and the transcendent while staying away from and rejecting what we perceive as nonpractice, worldly activities. What we associate with practice and the nonworldly is often derived from our experience in residential silent meditation retreats. The simple living environment, daily routine, and requirement to refrain from social interactions provide an artificial environment conducive to settling the mind for a concentrated period of practice. Our attachment to the quietude in this period of practice drives us to view "worldly" activities with disdain. We are worried that engaging in "worldly" activities might defile the "pure mind" we have worked so hard to cultivate.

It is true that some activities are harmful for our body and mind, and to refrain from them is a wise choice. But when we define all but a narrow range of activities as nonpractice and worldly, we may want to check to see if we are creating a separation between ourselves and everyone else—the cave constructed to protect us from the world. Living a simple life is not in itself dwelling in quietism. When causes and conditions make our life more complicated, do we embrace it as an opportunity to practice and learn new things, or do we resist it and try to go back to our simple life as soon as possible? If it's the latter, we may be attached to quietism, and it is advisable to check to see if we are doing so in our meditation.

THE PRACTICE AND ENGAGEMENT IN THE WORLD ARE COMPATIBLE!

The mindset that compels us to become attached to quietism also leads us to believe that the outside world is dangerous. We may work hard to construct a safe haven to protect ourselves against this world that we perceive to be defiled. For some, that safe haven may be meditation or a Dharma center or other spiritual community. Again, it is important to remember that there is nothing inherently problematic with practicing meditation and being involved in a Dharma community per se. We benefit from the cultivation of awareness of our thoughts and feelings in relation to other practitioners. However, do we believe that it is an absolutely safe and pure place where nothing problematic can happen? Are we turning our Dharma center (or whatever safe haven we have chosen) into the dark cave that provides the illusion of safety from the "dangerous world" outside? In other words, are we hiding from the world? Are we maintaining this illusion of safety by covering our eyes and ears, by shutting down our awareness, including to some of what is happening in this "safe" haven?

We need to remember that, while nearly everyone has come to practice, Dharma communities comprise ordinary human beings who are habituated to craving and aversion and self-centered attachment. We try our best to be compassionate, yet we will still cause harm to others from time to time when our practice slips and we succumb to our entrenched habits of suffering. Blindly believing *any* place is absolutely safe and shutting down our natural capacity for clear awareness and discernment is not wisdom.

Holding on to the idea of the world being dangerous to justify hiding in our chosen safe haven is also not illumination because we are cultivating a distorted view of the world. In this view, the problems of the "dangers" outside of us are exaggerated and we ignore the positive aspects. Conversely, the positive aspects of our chosen safe haven are exaggerated while the problems are ignored and dismissed. When we cultivate total clear awareness of the world as it is, without distortion by our prejudgment, we will notice conflict, greed, and violence as well as kindness, generosity, community spirit, and love—in both our safe haven and the wider world. When we release our attachment to the need for a safe haven, we allow ourselves to see our spiritual community as it is—not good, not bad—just a space devoted to the Dharma cocreated by human beings trying their best to live and make sense of this life. Practicing this way, we can clearly see that a supportive spiritual community is a place where we can be vulnerable and honest with ourselves, learn from our mistakes, and grow in wisdom and compassion. It is not a place to hide from the world.

RETURNING TO SILENT ILLUMINATION

Our attachment to quietude may lead us to believe that emotional engagement with others is dangerous for our practice. Related to this is the belief that the feeling of love or emotional connection might disturb or destroy the peace we have worked so hard to build and protect. With this belief, we may fulfill our responsibilities by performing tasks associated with our role—as a provider, housekeeper, caregiver, problem-solver, helping hand—but resist being emotionally available. Our family and close friends would like us to love them, to be there with them to experience the pain and joy of life together, to open our hearts and be fully present so they feel loved. If we abide in quietude and come to believe emotional engagement is dangerous, we are not allowing the emotions of love and connection to touch our hearts for fear they will disturb our peace. Not only do we deprive ourselves of love and connection, but we also make our loved ones feel unloved.

The dark cave is an apt description of the habit of quietism. It is as if we go into a dark cave isolated from the rest of the world emotionally, believing that the darkness—the lack of exposure and emotional connection to others—is the peace in which we can abide. This is not in accordance with compassion because people in our life feel unloved and rejected for reasons they do not understand. When we do not allow ourselves to be touched by emotional pain and joy in life, we cannot truly empathize when others need our support. Quietism is not in accordance with wisdom. We cocreate the world with others and are interdependent. To believe that we can separate ourselves from the "defiled" world and dwell in our "pure" cave untouched by the world is to forget that we are interconnected. We are not fully alive as we cut ourselves off from the world and from our emotions. Instead of freeing ourselves from suffering, we imprison ourselves in the dark cave.

Whether you are in the cave or in the process of entering, keep an eye on habitual thoughts as you react to situations in your life. If you notice you have forgotten that we are all interconnected, and your mind is setting up opposites and taking sides, bring up clarity to stay with each moment as it is. As we reconnect with our existence and its flow of causes and conditions, the powerful urge to hold up the wall of our cave is released. Moment after moment, as we cultivate clear awareness in Silent Illumination, the walls melt like ice under the summer sun.

12

FORGETTING-EMPTINESS MODE
Resisting the True Nature of Reality

Forgetting emptiness is an entrenched habit. It is perpetuated by the subtle belief, irrational as it may be, that there is some-place, something that is permanent that we can abide in and rely upon. When we believe we have found it, we stop being fully here; we have disconnected from the emerging present moment. We forget that this moment—the unique coming to-gether of constantly changing causes and conditions—is all there is and become prone to reifying an experience or the self. We get in the way of our natural capacity to fully engage with life as it unfolds.

I once met a practitioner who felt that he was practicing very well when he had a summer off from work and spent his mornings and evenings meditating. During the day he read Dharma books, spent time in nature, and painted and drew. He felt that he was deepening his practice, and in many ways he was, but as soon as he returned to work things fell apart. He got busy, stressed, and exhausted. He could no longer maintain the calmness, stability, and clarity he achieved before his work resumed. He said he could hardly bring himself to meditate, and when he did, his mind was so noisy with all the things going on at his job that he wondered what the point was. What was the purpose of sitting when his mind was so noisy, his thoughts so busy?

Does this sound familiar? Perhaps you have had a period when you felt your practice was really strong, you were able to meditate well regularly, and you were pleased with your practice. Then suddenly circumstances changed, and you couldn't meditate as much; it took longer to settle your mind down, leading you to believe you lost your practice. We get frustrated, bemoaning how life gets in the way of practice. What is going on here is that your frustration is a resentment of circumstances in the present moment. But our lives are not obstacles. When we encounter circumstances that give us more space in life and allow us to practice meditation while we are relatively relaxed and happy, we tend to think, "I got it. I am a good practitioner. I finally figured out how to practice." Along with this thought is the belief that this is now the state of one's life. We tell ourselves, "I have turned over a new leaf!" assuming the "new me" has replaced the "old me." It's as if we bought a new car or computer and as a result thought everything would be great from that moment on. Because of impermanence, circumstances change—when work gets busy or relationships get challenging, we become stressed and prone to our entrenched habit of vexations. We may become disappointed that we haven't completely left our unhelpful habits behind.

For experienced practitioners, it is important to pay attention when thinking, "My practice is really strong. I finally figured out how to meditate well and am in a good place." Check to see if you are also thinking, "I am really getting close to enlightenment." This is an indication that you have forgotten that every moment is empty, and you have come to believe there is a place, or a particular state, you can abide in. It is a feeling like "I found a way to be peaceful, so let me just be at peace from now on." And perhaps you do meditate a lot and frequently attend retreats, which is great! It means you are familiar with the practice and the teaching, and you are proficient in the method of meditation. But whether you have been sitting for a lifetime or an hour, the question remains the same: Have you ever before been in this particular moment with this unique combination of conditions, thoughts, bodily sensations, and emotions?

Never.

Accepting each moment as a brand-new moment is what is meant by beginner's mind. What you are experiencing may be similar to what you have experienced before, but it is not the same. You are a different person with a different set of sensations and circumstances and even though it feels the same, when you really allow yourself to pay attention, you will notice you have never been in this exact moment before. Since all the components that cocreate this emerging present moment are constantly changing, this particular combination will not come together again either. We have never been in this particular emerging present moment before and never will be again. *Beginner's mind.*

Forgetting beginner's mind is an easy trap to fall into. You may believe that you have been in this moment before because it feels similar to a moment in the past. Or perhaps you are sitting in meditation and following your breath and even though you tell yourself it is a new breath, you really do not believe it and think, "It feels like the same breath over and over again." Or you begin to ruminate and think, "The same thoughts show up over and over again." What we are telling ourselves is that we already know this breath and already know this thought, and we do not need to be fully here; we do not need to pay full attention to this emerging present moment and see truly how it is a coming together of causes and conditions. When we do this, when we forget beginner's mind, we are actually forgetting emptiness, forgetting the true nature of reality.

TO FORGET EMPTINESS IS
TO GENERATE SUFFERING

When I worked with the practitioner who was having trouble returning to his job and "real" life, I pointed out to him that the challenges at the office and within his family combined with health issues and tiring commutes may appear to be overwhelming, and so the mind is busier. However, we can be at peace amid the rapidly changing causes and conditions. When so much is going on at once, we may think something is wrong, but there is nothing wrong. When we see this is life unfolding as causes and conditions come together, we understand what emptiness is.

Every moment, peaceful or busy, clear or confused, is emptiness. When we pick and choose, saying, "I do not like this emptiness, I like that other emptiness better," we generate suffering for ourselves. In the practice of Silent Illumination there is no selecting a certain emptiness and abiding only in that. We stay with this just as this, moment after moment.

As we remember to give rise to beginner's mind, to not fall into the habits of forgetting or resisting emptiness, we'll see that this beginner's mind is really the mind of not knowing. It is not the mind of "I have it all figured out. I do not need to really pay attention to this moment because I already know." Having not-knowing mind does not mean you are an idiot, deliberately becoming dull, but rather seeing each emerging moment as brand-new and being fully present for its unfolding. It is allowing total clear awareness and experiencing each emerging moment directly and fully without falling into any of the modes of operation.

Not-knowing mind is important because without it we forget and resist emptiness—we ignore the true nature of reality and generate suffering. Instead, we should remember the Buddha's teaching, "This arises, that arises." When vexation arises, suffering arises. "When this perishes, that perishes." When vexation does not arise, suffering does not arise. We must be fully present with it all.

COMPLACENT, DULL, AND FLAVORLESS PRACTICE

If you have practiced for a long time, pay attention to thoughts like "I've practiced for thirty years. I sit every day. I already know this." This attitude of believing that "I already know what happens in meditation" is a subtle thought that leads us to stop paying full attention.

We may be paying attention, but not fully. It is like when our parent tells a story we have heard many times before—we start listening, but our attention wanes. Some words or entire sentences are unheard even though we appear to be listening.

We allow our awareness to dull because we believe we already know the story. When we forget that this is a brand-new moment, we may miss the message being conveyed, perhaps our parent's love or worry, as they recount this story. Our practice includes noticing the moment when our awareness dulls. We may not be deliberately dulling the mind; the subtle attitude of already knowing makes our attention lax. We may also believe that we can rely on our past accumulated practice experience. This is of course an erroneous view. We have never been in this moment before and never will be again; it is impossible to already know. This subtle attitude of thinking "I already know" encourages us to be complacent, providing an opening for our ingrained modes of operation to slip in and take over.

Perhaps we feel our practice is getting a bit stale, so we begin looking for something other than the present moment to engage us. Because we believe we already know, thinking "I am an experienced meditator," our mind is not fully engaged with what is arising in each moment. Without this clear awareness, meditation feels like the same old blah routine. There is no sense of the curiosity of beginner's mind to help us stay fully and clearly engaged in every moment. We may begin to look for or create something more interesting to entertain us in our meditation. What happens is, because of this attitude of believing we already know, we are not convinced we need to be fully here in every moment. It is a complacency in practice, believing we can lean on past moments of practice. It is like saying, "I don't need to look at the road when I drive because I have driven this route many times before." Instead of cultivating clear awareness of each brand-new moment, we venture into something we believe to be more profound or more enlightening. As we take this moment for granted and look around for other meditative experiences, we perpetuate the habit of feeling that what is right now is not good enough, and that is suffering.

I have met practitioners who have fallen into complacency in the practice of Silent Illumination and are looking for something more interesting. Having heard that the huatou method of meditation can be quite powerful, some have asked me if they could begin meditating with a question or koan. It is true that huatou, which involves sustained concentration on a particular question, is an effective method. But if you forget the beginner's mind, you will find the huatou questions grow stale in the same way when the novelty wears off. In the practice of Silent Illumination, notice these subtle thoughts of not feeling convinced that you truly need to be fully here moment after moment. As soon as you detect the shift into complacency that allows your awareness to dull, remind yourself of the beginner's mind and bring up this clear awareness of each emerging present moment as brand-new.

ATTACHING TO WHAT
WE ALREADY KNOW

The idea "I've already got it" leads us to believe that we don't need to be fully here and obscures from us the total clear awareness of what *is* right here. If we allow ourselves to be fully engaged, clearly aware, we will notice that whatever is in this moment is wondrous and alive.

The mode of forgetting emptiness shows up in life through this habit of attaching to what we already know. When we start to feel our bodies age and begin to practice with the experience of aging, we may believe, "Aging . . . Yes, I've experienced that. I have practiced with it. I can see emptiness and impermanence. I know what aging is." Because we believe we already know, we stop paying full attention to the continually unfolding process of aging as it is and how it shows up in our lived experience moment to moment. As a result, we do not see what is really going on and can be blindsided when we discover the body can no longer do certain things. Suddenly, we realize how challenging or difficult aging is. Even though the body has been showing signs of wear and tear, we haven't been truly paying attention because we believed we already knew aging. It is not so much that we were intellectualizing as that we leaned on certain past experiences and understandings. We may realize that we are aging in our forties: "Oh. I know. It takes longer to recover from an all-nighter. This is aging. I already got it." Yet the experience of aging changes as we advance in age. If we keep thinking that's all there is to aging and do not pay attention to how the body and mind change over the years, we will encounter a big surprise. When things don't work out because we cannot function the way we used to, without this clear awareness, we resort to blame and being angry with the world, causing suffering for ourselves and others.

REIFYING EXPERIENCE

When we forget emptiness, we are prone to reifying experience— treating it as if it were permanent and concrete. We may reify meditation practice as taking a certain form. My use of the phrase "cultivating clear awareness" may give the impression that we can achieve this thing called clear awareness. It really doesn't matter what word or phrase we use; this mode has to do with our habit of trying to reify that which is a constantly changing process into a fixed entity. If we have a moment of clarity, our inclination may be to think, "Oh, yes. This is clarity that I have. That is it." And we want to freeze it and preserve it in our minds, to possess it and rely on it.

A student of mine often complained that she could not find clarity in her practice—she didn't believe it was really there, and this had become a real problem for her. We may use different words to describe this, but we are forgetting emptiness when we believe the experience of clarity is a sign that the practice is going well and want to capture and make permanent certain moments of our experience, saying, "This is it. I can lean on that and rely on this moment." We forget that every moment is the coming together of changing causes and conditions. There is not a moment whatsoever we can abide in.

Underlying this desire to gain something in the practice is the habitual tendency to see the practice as a means to an end. We imagine a prize is waiting for us at the end of this hard work, something other than this moment, and we forget what the Heart Sutra tells us: there is nothing to attain. By contrast, our erroneous view stems from the belief that there is something to attain, a certain insight or experience to hold on to, and that we should always be able to rely on it being exactly that way for us. In fact, enlightenment is already here in this moment. To realize this, we need to get out of our own way. Silent Illumination is a practice of letting go of our entrenched habit of grasping; all we need to do is to be fully here. Many times, at the end of a Silent Illumination retreat Master Sheng Yen would say, "If you leave the retreat feeling that you have gained something, then something is wrong." Remember this when you fall into the habit of reifying experience. There is nothing to attain.

This habit can be subtle. We may not broadcast our perceived attainment but, in our minds, we think, "That's it! Oh, I got this." It is a sign that we have fallen into this habit of forgetting emptiness, an entrenched habit of wanting to be able to find a place that we can abide in for security and safety. With the realization that everything is conditioned and that there is nothing permanent on which we can rely—that there is only this moment—comes the motivation to be fully present with each moment as it is. The Dharma tells us that there is nothing we can rely on, nothing we can abide in, not even the Dharma—everything is interconnected and constantly changing.

MISUNDERSTANDING EMPTINESS: IT IS NOT NIHILISM

Shunyata (emptiness) is sometimes translated as "nothingness," which may lead to a misperception that the practice is about nihilism. This couldn't be further from the truth. Nihilism can show up when there is a strong desire to hold on to something—a feeling, a relationship, anything. After learning that everything is impermanent and that every moment is emptiness, one can slip into thinking, "What is the point in doing anything if nothing lasts?" "The point" in this sense is something on to which we try to hold. When we hear that nothing is permanent, we interpret that as "there is no point," conveying the disillusionment with the idea that there is nothing to hold on to.

Emptiness does not mean that nothing exists. This moment certainly exists and is very much real. Yet we do not let ourselves fully live and engage in this emerging present moment when we are too busy trying to look for a permanent moment. We are taking this moment for granted and judging it for how we think it should be, and we end up missing the wondrous life that is unfolding around us. When we do not fall in the habit of forgetting emptiness, we are actually living a fully engaged life. It is not nihilistic. Instead, we can see a lot of hope. It is hopeful in the sense that what we do in this moment will touch future moments.

It is particularly important to keep this in mind when we despair, thinking that all is lost or there is no hope. Everything we do in this moment is cocreating the world. However small it seems, it touches the people around you, and they, in turn, touch other people. We have no idea how much we affect others with as little as one thought or action. Remember: "This arises, that arises."

"I DO NOT BELIEVE YOU WILL LIKE IT"

There is a story that when someone asked Zen Master Shunryū Suzuki, "What is enlightenment?" he replied, "Enlightenment? I do not believe you will like it." The enlightenment to which he was referring is fully accepting that everything without any exception is empty and impermanent. That means there is no single thing we can abide in. Whatever it is that we think we've gotten or achieved in practice (or in life, because life is practice) cannot be held on to or relied on to give us advance knowledge of this brand-new moment. We need to be fully here to directly experience each moment.

This may sound like a lot of work, but actually, we are naturally capable of being fully here, if we just stop getting in the way of ourselves by wishing that there was one thing we could discover and grasp as permanent and then be done having to do any work in our lives or our practice. Think about it like paddleboarding. When we stand on the paddleboard we need to be balanced and fully alert to the moving water, moment after moment after moment. If when we can stand up for a few seconds, we think, "I got it," that is when we fall into the water. We lose contact with the emerging present moment by trying to hold on to it as if there is one correct position that we can remain in. To stay on the board, we have to constantly alter our body's position as water moves under the board, even if subtly. No moment is the same.

One manifestation of the mode of forgetting emptiness is thinking "All I need to do is to get enlightened, then all my problems will be solved." Enlightenment experience allows us to realize emptiness through direct experience. It strengthens our faith in this path of practice. We still need to continue to practice unlearning our entrenched unhelpful habits as we engage in each new moment. Practitioners habituated to this mode may also notice this way of thinking in their daily life, recognizing thought patterns like "If only I could find a partner and get married, I would be happy!" or "All I need is to get this promotion, then I will be set." Perhaps what is causing you stress now may no longer be an issue after you achieve these goals. However, seeing these achievements as the be-all and end-all of life is forgetting emptiness. This can lead us to stop being fully present and engaged, mistakenly believing that our work in this relationship or at this job is complete, which will eventually cause suffering for ourselves and others.

Another manifestation of this mode is the habit of waiting—

waiting for enlightenment to happen. Waiting for enlightenment is a habit of forgetting emptiness because we believe, "I am doing this so that some emptiness, some enlightenment, will show up." And what is it that you think will show up? You are not even here to fully experience this moment! This habit of waiting has to do with the habit of reifying the idea of future moments that we would like to attain and believe are not accessible now. Again, we are forgetting that everything is just this moment and, because we forget that, we are not fully here. If you fall into this mode, you will be waiting for enlightenment forever.

FORGETTING EMPTINESS IN LIFE

When we forget emptiness, we forget that life is dynamic. Causes and conditions are constantly changing, and we must stay with each emerging present moment. Just like surfing on the ocean, we need to be ready to turn the body in the opposite direction and pivot again in split seconds as the wave changes. Yet that is not how we behave in life. We tend to turn ourselves into a fixed person in our relationships. When we are with a child, for instance, do we turn ourselves into "the adult" who knows everything? Maybe we are the parent or teacher or aunt, and we believe we should be the one teaching the child all the time. When we turn ourselves into a fixed person, we miss the chance to learn from the child's keen observations and unique perspective. Instead of letting them also teach us in this moment, we believe we already know what they know. If we're being the adult who knows, we won't listen to them and enter their world, and hence we'll miss the opportunity to connect with them more deeply. We may also be so attached to being the adult that we can't relax and really play with the child. But when we remember emptiness, we realize that we cocreate each moment with this child. We stay with each emerging present moment as it unfolds. One moment, we teach the child something. The next moment, we ask the child to help us figure something out. In the next moment, we get out the toys and just play. When we are done playing, we can work together with the child to clean up. We realize that there is no "adult who knows" residing in us permanently.

Another way that forgetting emptiness shows up in our lives is when we reify the practice as taking a certain form and move through life with a fixed self-entity such as "I am a serious practitioner." No matter what situation we are in, the "I am a serious practitioner" identity shows up in the way we talk, stand, carry ourselves, or interact with others. We may be doing this to tell ourselves, "I am really practicing well here. I am above all this." This behavior has to do with the belief that being a serious practitioner, having a good practice, or being awake takes a certain form. It means "I have to behave in a certain way" or "I must always talk about profound Dharma concepts such as emptiness." In this sort of mindset, living in Dharma is to say those words and talk about the practice all the time. Chan is formless, so we do not need to discuss our practice with people who are not interested in or ready for these teachings. Instead, be fully connected and engaged with everyone you encounter; if someone in line at the grocery store wants to chat about how cold the weather is, talk to them about the weather. This is also the practice of Silent Illumination. When we have an idea that Silent Illumination takes a certain form, then that idea gets in the way of full engagement in the emerging present moment. That is what happens when we forget emptiness. As soon as you catch yourself falling into the habit of forgetting emptiness, reconnect with the practice and give rise to the beginner's mind.

RETURNING TO SILENT ILLUMINATION

We may also become attached to the forms or rituals of the practice. There are many different things we may use as tools or guideposts in the process of practice, like keeping to a schedule, going to retreats, or meditating daily. Those are helpful, but we need to remember their function is to help us practice. They are part of practicing, not the practice itself. As soon as we establish in our mind, "This is how Dharma manifests in the world," we set up a duality compelling us to attach to that which is Dharma and reject that which is not Dharma. Then we might judge our practice or the practice of others if these specific forms are not followed. That is when we give rise to suffering.

This is attachment to the Dharma itself that the Diamond Sutra warns us about:

> So you should not be attached to things as being possessed of, or devoid of, intrinsic qualities.
> This is the reason why the Tathagata always teaches this saying: My teaching of the good law is to be likened unto a raft. The buddha-teaching must be relinquished; how much more so mis-teaching![15]

You need the raft when you are going across the river but be careful not to become so attached to the raft that you are still trying to hold on to it while on land after you reach the other shore. Forgetting emptiness is believing the raft is our abode. There is no permanent abode.

Certain things we do in the practice are to help us be here, to stay connected to the present moment. But when we believe that we cannot practice outside of that form, that is when we get into trouble. Actually, I met someone who, when she couldn't attend in-person retreats during the COVID-19 pandemic because retreat centers were closed, refused to join online retreats, thinking "that is not the *real* practice." She suffered greatly during the first year of the pandemic. When she finally decided to sign up for an online retreat, she realized that it was her attachment to a certain idea of the form, to what the real practice should look like, that caused her suffering. Whenever we think of anything as having a fixed form, we are forgetting emptiness.

Shunryū Suzuki Roshi has been quoted as saying, "Life is like stepping onto a boat that is about to sail out to sea and sink." We are always thinking that we are going somewhere, but we are not. This points to our habit of waiting for enlightenment as if we are practicing for something in the future. We are conditioned in our society to think this way: you sit so that you can calm your mind, your mind becomes calm, you get enlightened. But as long as you think, "I am sitting here waiting for the mind to become calm," then this waiting is directing you to look forward instead of being fully here. Enlightenment is already here, but we think it is somewhere else and that it is supposed to look like something else. Everything we experience is going to change. Like a sinking boat, this moment will be gone. Yet the point of life is to step in and fully experience the journey, moment to moment.

At the beginning of a meditation session, John Crook often said, "Make your mind bright," reminding us to bring up total clear awareness. This is good advice, yet often we don't make our minds bright and instead use the word *bright* to reify our preexisting notions. If we are looking for "experiences" in our meditation, we might think, "Oh practice is about seeing a lot of bright light." I have heard students say things like "Oh, yeah. It is just like that. This brightness. This brightness in the room. This is it." Seeking something to hold on to we end up reifying clarity as if it is a thing we can capture in a bottle in our mind. When you make your mind bright moment after moment, there is no brightness to behold. Every moment we remember to practice, remembering emptiness, the mind is bright—simply illuminating the present. Of course, this is an entrenched habit; we will forget emptiness. The mind will seek to reify. When we forget emptiness, it's not a problem. Just come back to the practice and release the habit of grasping for something to abide in. Remind yourself that there is no need for that. Every moment is our abode. We just need to be here.

Words and concepts are useful tools but beware of the tendency to be trapped by them, by ideas or beliefs that are created by your mind. Master Sheng Yen said that Silent Illumination is about letting go—letting go of the habit of getting trapped by thoughts and words. It is not a matter of making them go away but releasing the entrenched habit of grasping on to those thoughts and words. When we remember this, the practice is formless. That is why Silent Illumination is the method of no-method. No matter what we are doing in the present moment—sitting on a cushion with thoughts arising or hugging a loved one in a moment of grief or joy—we can practice Silent Illumination.

13

ALLOWING WHAT IS AND
BEING FULLY HERE

As you have seen, there are many modes of operation that practitioners fall into when reacting to what happens in the present moment instead of allowing that moment to be fully experienced as it is. My intention in this book is to help you begin to pay attention to the direct experience of your body and mind in this space. As the mind settles and we begin to penetrate it, we see its subtle movements more clearly. When we do so, we realize that by being *fully* here we can experience how we get in the way of ourselves, how we obscure our full connection to each emerging present moment and thus to life.

I use the phrase "being fully here" to point to the cultivation of total clear awareness in the practice of Silent Illumination. It is important to remember that in this practice, what we are doing is truly allowing the entirety of our body/mind/environment to be as it is moment to moment. When we do this, we cultivate wisdom and compassion on the Buddhist path. As we engage in the practice, we begin by realizing the first noble truth, as pointed out to us by Shakyamuni Buddha:

we suffer. Even people who have heard this teaching many times can continue to resist or deny the fact of suffering—our habit of being unsatisfied with whatever is happening in the present moment, resisting life unfolding as it is. The present moment + vexation = suffering. As we practice Silent Illumination, we come to realize this truth of suffering and how our suffering affects other people. This realization is essential—it proves to us that we need to practice.

The Buddha describes suffering as a disease of the mind and his teaching the medicine. If we do not acknowledge that we are sick, we will not take our medicine because we do not believe we need it. Likewise, if we are not convinced that practice is necessary and even essential, we will not be motivated to do sitting meditation, or when we do, we fall asleep or distract or delude ourselves while we sit. If you struggle with these issues in your meditation practice, I recommend looking into your mind and asking yourself honestly if you are fully convinced you need to practice. If the answer is no, then you have not realized how much you suffer.

The solution to this is to return to the practice again and again because when we allow the mind to settle, we have the opportunity to see for ourselves the myriad ways in which we are unsatisfied with the present moment as it is, of how we create all of our own suffering. We notice habits of thinking, "It is not good enough" or "It is not how it is supposed to be" or "I'd rather be doing something else and be somewhere else," and on and on it goes. This is the disease of the mind that the Buddha's teachings are meant to cure. We realize that we are quite good at finding fault with the present moment. This is an important realization.

The Buddha's teachings offer us a promise that we can suffer less and ultimately bring an end to the habit of suffering. In the beginning, we may not be convinced. Do not just take my word for it, or Master Sheng Yen's, or any teacher's—test the teachings by putting them to use in your life and see if they work. Think of it as an experiment. Chances are you will notice that in the moments when you remember to practice and are fully in the present moment, you won't suffer much even in the most challenging situations. You will also notice that when you forget or neglect to practice because the mind is scattered and agitated, you suffer a lot even if you are not in a particularly challenging situation.

Many practitioners grow frustrated with themselves when they fall out of the practice, seeing it as a failure. Instead of further agitating the mind by judging it as a failure, which of course leads to more suffering, we can use these moments to deepen our understanding and appreciation of the Buddha's teachings. When we remember to practice, less suffering will arise; when we forget to practice, more suffering arises. Seeing this helps us remember the importance of taking the medicine, of choosing and remembering to practice in this moment so as not to generate more suffering. This is what is meant by wisdom.

THE PURPOSE OF PRACTICE IS TO RECOGNIZE OUR MODES OF OPERATION

As we recognize that we suffer, it is crucial that we also pay attention to the myriad ways in which we cause that suffering. Most of us believe other people are the problem and focus on changing or even eliminating these people from their lives. The truth of the matter is that the present moment is the coming together of many causes and conditions. We create suffering when we refuse to accept this. Remember, by "accepting," I do not mean telling ourselves that what is going on in the present moment is right, good, how it is supposed to be, or what we deserve. That is not what is meant by accepting. Accepting is facing and recognizing what is happening as it is. This is quite difficult to do, especially if it violates our beliefs and assumptions of how the world should work. It is in this reaction, this disbelief, that we activate the modes of operation to resist the fact of what is happening. We may crave a different moment, declare war against this moment or pretend it is not happening, dwell in the world of intellectual concepts as a substitute for directly experiencing the moment, or attach to our idea of emptiness. As you have seen in the previous chapters, this is not an exhaustive list of possible modes of operation; as you cultivate your practice and discover and work with one, you are likely to discover another and yet another.

Many practitioners get frustrated with themselves when they recognize that most if not all the modes of operation apply to them. Sometimes, they are even a bit horrified, especially those who have taken their practice seriously, are dedicated, and believe they've been practicing diligently. Master Sheng Yen taught that "it is normal for cultivators to discover their vexations. If you do not discover vexations in the course of cultivating your practice, you are having problems. The clearer you are about the activities of your mind, the lighter the obstructions become."[16] What Master Sheng Yen said may seem counterintuitive. In fact, if you are not discovering your vexations—the way you habitually react to situations—you are not paying attention to the activities of the mind. Vexations show up because they are entrenched habits of ours, but there is no need to declare war against them. We simply need to remember to continue to cultivate clear awareness of how these habitual tendencies show up and unfold moment after moment as we respond to every situation. When we remember to practice this way, we do not fall into the habit of reacting to and hating our vexations (which only causes more suffering) and instead can see them as thoughts that arise and perish and choose not to believe in them, not to live by them. Be prepared to see yourself getting upset when you notice this! After all, our default mode is to resist and give rise to aversion to reality as it is.

WHAT HAPPENS WHEN WE START SEEING CLEARLY?

In the initial phase of our practice, we may notice that we have reacted with our unhelpful habits but are unable to see how it happened. With the cultivation of total clear awareness in Silent Illumination, as the mind settles, we can see more clearly how these habits emerge and unfold thought after thought. We gain insight into our desires and how they compel us to activate the various unhelpful modes of operation in reaction to the emerging present moment. We can see directly for ourselves how each thought is conditioned by another because we see each thought as it is, nothing but thoughts, as temporary as clouds and lightning in the sky, soap bubbles or shadow—they are without inherent and independent existence. In this way we cultivate insight into the true nature of existence, that each moment is the coming together of causes and conditions that are constantly changing.

Remember what John Crook often said: "Chan is not supposed to be comfortable." *Indeed.* Seeing all the ways in which we cause suffering for ourselves and others is difficult and challenging. You should give yourself credit for persevering, even if you need to take breaks from time to time. Many people get too disturbed by the discomfort and quit, often because they only focus on the discomfort and overlook the implications of their discovery. When we can see clearly for ourselves that it is our habitual reactivity to the present moment that causes suffering, it means we are able to unlearn these unhelpful habits. This is incredibly empowering! We no longer need to try to change other people. We can stop giving rise to the vexations we discover. In each moment, we realize we can stop perpetuating any mode of operation that is unfolding and live a fully engaged life without the unhelpful habits of suffering.

Chan practice is a lifelong process as we continuously work with ourselves to clearly see how we generate our own suffering. In the beginning, we are likely to discover the more obvious ways in which we cause suffering for ourselves. At first these are the gross-level vexations like becoming irritated by what is going on or wishing we were somewhere else doing something else. With a little effort, these can be readily recognized. As we practice more and keep penetrating the mind, we become able to see more clearly how these unhelpful habitual tendencies manifest themselves as more subtle thought patterns and ubiquitous beliefs about the world that shape our perception. These beliefs are often deep-rooted, conditioned by the social and cultural environment from which we came and in which we live.

As we make these realizations, John Crook's instruction to "let through, let be, let go" is worth keeping in mind. As you may recall, "let through" refers to allowing the thoughts that are already in our mind to be there without blocking or fighting against them, which agitates the mind. When the mind is agitated, there is little clarity. Vexations in the form of habitual reactivities are already part of the present moment when they enter our awareness; hating them will not undo them even if we believe otherwise. In our attempt to block vexations from our awareness, not only do we not stop causing suffering, but we also deprive ourselves of the opportunity to see clearly how this habit is operating and obscuring the present moment. When we remember to let be, we allow the vexation, manifesting in an unfolding of thoughts and emotions, to be fully experienced and seen as it is. We are not fueling vexations with more vexations, not reacting to aversion with aversion. When vexations are seen clearly as mere thoughts, even though there is a compulsive quality to them, they lose their power. Like all thoughts, they dissipate and move on, and we let go.

Remember, Master Sheng Yen said that the practice of Silent Illumination is the process of letting go. This phrase is often misunderstood as forcefully eliminating or making thought go away. Rather it is a process of waking up to how we cause suffering by giving rise to these unhelpful habitual tendencies which we believe, misguidedly, will provide what we want. When we see how unhelpful and destructive these habitual tendencies are, and how they get in the way of our being able to fully engage in life, we realize that we no longer have to perpetuate these habitual tendencies. We can allow the emerging present moment to be Silent Illumination.

As we practice this way, the habitual tendency to react to the present moment with various modes of operation is gradually unlearned and released. The mind becomes still as we are no longer agitating the mind with habitual reactivity to the present moment. With this clarity and stillness, we are more able to see that in every moment there is a choice for us to not perpetuate the habit of suffering. We remember to choose not to perpetuate the habit of suffering by not succumbing to these entrenched modes of operation. Not causing suffering is *wisdom*. With this clarity, we see we are truly interdependent with all sentient beings; benefiting and loving others is no different from benefiting and loving ourselves—and with this wisdom, *compassion* arises naturally.

BEYOND THE MEDITATION CUSHION

People tend to believe that Chan is only about sitting meditation. Indeed, for many of us, sitting meditation is where we start to learn about the mind as we attempt to calm it. However it is not the only place where Chan practice happens. Practicing Chan means to live life fully with this body and mind in each moment as it is.

There is so much going on in each moment for an untrained mind that this seemingly simple instruction may feel overwhelming. Sitting meditation provides a simplified setting for us to learn to settle the mind by working with a meditation method as we gain insight into the habitual tendencies that are activated in response to experiences of the body and mind. I like to use the analogy of learning how to drive to help us understand why we sit in meditation. We often learn how to drive in an empty parking lot. The simplified environment without active traffic or nearby pedestrians allows us to familiarize ourselves with the vehicle. We can see what happens when we push the gas pedal and brake gently or abruptly and learn to monitor the rearview and side mirrors without losing sight of the road ahead. Similarly, during sitting meditation our life is simplified by refraining from social interaction and by setting up the body in a stable posture conducive to relaxation. We learn how to work with ourselves to rest our attention gently on the meditation method without generating tension. We also learn how to find our way back to the method when the mind drifts off and to practice remembering to do so over and over again without losing patience. We become familiar with our modes of operation that are triggered when the mind is busy or drowsy and when bodily discomfort develops. We practice driving in an empty parking lot to learn how to handle the vehicle proficiently so that we can drive safely on a busy highway. We do not learn to drive in a parking lot just to keep driving only in a parking lot. We practice in sitting meditation to settle the mind and to gain insight into our habitual tendencies so that we can bring the practice to every aspect and every moment of our life.

As we become familiar with our habitual tendencies, we apply what we learn in sitting meditation to our moment-to-moment practice in daily life. When we do so, we are likely to notice that the very same modes of operation activated when we experience physical or mental discomfort in sitting meditation tend to also show up in daily life when we encounter challenging situations. For example, if we create a foggy mind to avoid experiencing uncomfortable emotions, we are likely to find ourselves turning away and hiding in denial when conflict and painful emotions arise in daily life. Similarly, we will notice that our favorite modes of operation that are activated when sitting meditation is pleasant also show up when things are going well in life. If we crave a rerun of a blissful meditation session, we may find ourselves with the tendency to be dissatisfied with the present situation in life while wishing to go back to some wonderful moment from the past. We are not doing sitting meditation to become expert sitting meditators. We sit in meditation to provide a simplified setting to learn to live life moment after moment as it is—to see for ourselves how we get in our way of doing so and to unlearn these unhelpful habits. The insight into our mind that we gain in sitting meditation helps us see more clearly how we have been generating our suffering by activating these unhelpful habitual tendencies often without being aware of our doing so. We must carry that knowledge and skill into the rest of our life.

BEING FULLY HUMAN

Living life as a human being with this body and mind can be challenging. We experience happiness and sadness. We experience health and vigor, but also our bodies get sick, deteriorate with age, and die. All of these experiences are the *being* in "human being" and it is all as natural as blossoms blooming, withering, and falling from a tree. Our resistance to the impermanence of the body causes suffering, perhaps manifesting in ideas like "This is not how it is supposed to be." We may accept conceptually that it is natural for humans to age and die, but we secretly wish that we and our loved ones would be exempt. Instead of being with life as it is, we suffer.

Living as a human being, we naturally feel emotional pain when we are separated from our loved ones because we have a heart and are not inanimate objects. We hold different views about the world owing to our different experiences—it is inevitable that we will work or live with someone who will disagree with or dislike us. As much as we want and work hard to achieve something, causes and conditions often bring together outcomes different from the ones we have in mind. Relationships change, situations change, people change.

Life as a human being is flowing, not fixed, and we never know for sure what will happen in the next moment. When we forget this and resist the true nature of life as it is, craving certainty and for pleasant moments to be permanent and hating that which does not match our ideal notion of the present moment, we suffer. When we practice Silent Illumination, we truly see for ourselves how we suffer and in our own ways resist the present moment as it is. This returns us to the realization of the first noble truth.

As the mind settles in Silent Illumination, we notice how we allow our habitual modes of operation to block us from seeing that each moment is the coming together of causes and conditions—how we perpetuate the habit of suffering. That is the realization of the second noble truth.

The good news is that the Buddha discovered that our habit of reacting with vexation is not hardwired. It is possible for us to train our mind to unlearn these habits and live a fully engaged life. We can have loving relationships and apply our talents to contribute to the world without generating suffering. This is because suffering, like all phenomena, is the coming together of causes and conditions. When vexation arises, suffering arises. When vexation ceases to arise, suffering ceases to arise. This is the third noble truth—cessation of suffering. It is important to remember this does not mean no misfortune will befall us. There will still be sickness, aging, and death, separation from loved ones, encountering those with whom we disagree, and not getting what we want. We will continue to experience the joy and pain of being human with this body and mind. And each moment we practice being fully present, not succumbing to the entrenched habit of nitpicking the present moment, vexation does not arise and suffering ceases.

Thus, the practice of Silent Illumination is the simultaneous cultivation of all eight components of the Eightfold Path, which is the fourth noble truth. It is to fully experience each moment of life as it is, with wisdom and compassion. In Silent Illumination, we see each unfolding present moment clearly as the coming together of causes and conditions (right view). We remember to be fully here with total clear awareness experiencing the present moment as it is—right concentration and mindfulness. Each moment we clearly see the habitual tendencies arising in response to what is going on, we work with ourselves skillfully to not perpetuate our habits of generating suffering (right diligence). This stability and clarity of mind allow us to become intimately familiar with the way the chain of subtle thoughts and feelings emerges and develops into speech and action. With clear awareness, we take care to not allow these habitual tendencies to materialize into harmful speech and action (right intention, right speech, right action, right livelihood).

Each moment we are in Silent Illumination and habits of vexation do not arise, suffering does not arise. As our practice becomes more proficient, we break the habitual thought chain earlier and earlier. Gradually, these patterns lose their power to compel us to act them out in our minds, bodies, or the world.

There is no need for us to declare war against vexations. With practice, they arise less often and with less power. Without giving rise to aversion to vexations, it no longer matters if these thought patterns show up or not. We can see them as no different from another fleeting thought and not give them power to control our life.

Practicing Silent Illumination in this way, we live fully—in equanimity and with open hearts. Eat when hungry. Rest when tired. Laugh when happy. Cry when sad. Not a problem.

ACKNOWLEDGMENTS

This book was cocreated by many people. The sincere practice of residential retreat participants at the Dharma Drum Retreat Center, Dharma Drum Vancouver Centre, Zen Mountain Monastery, and Western Chan Fellowship—as well as practitioners in the Chan Dharma Community—inspired the teachings that ended up in this book. Their willingness to engage in the practice earnestly—both in retreat and in their daily lives—and to share their difficulties honestly in interviews and written reports provided much of the inspiration for this book. The growth of so many of them through the practice gave me additional confidence that the method of Silent Illumination is worth sharing with more people, both Buddhists and non-Buddhists alike. If not for their sincere practice, these teachings would not have been given in the first place. My gratitude also goes to all the sanghas that invited me to teach and lead retreats.

Sumi Loundon Kim, my dear friend and fellow Dharma teacher, encouraged me to publish these teachings as a book and gave me useful advice on how to get started. Her encouragement planted the seed for this project. Many of my Gen X Dharma-teacher friends also inspired me with their books and supported me with their knowledge and encouragement. Their Dharma friendship has nourished and sustained me through the process.

My editor Alice Peck helped me envision the book and assemble the proposal, and she held my hand every step of the way throughout the writing process. I am deeply indebted to her for everything she did. I learned so much about writing and book publishing from her and feel blessed for her friendship. Her faith in and dedication to the project helped me understand why some authors rave about their editors. I don't think I have the words to do justice for my gratitude to Alice. Together, we lived through the pandemic and the loss of her dear friend, Ruth Mullen. I want to acknowledge Ruth's contribution to this book. She provided insightful feedback on the proposal and expressed enthusiasm that motivated me to stay with it despite health challenges. Even though she did not live to see the book published, her spirit stays with us.

I want to thank the Hemera Foundation for generously funding part of the expense incurred in writing this book. Thanks also go to my agent Stephanie Tade and her associate Ericka Phillips, who helped clarify the purpose of the book and find the right publisher. Many thanks to Casey Kemp, Peter Schumacher, Gretchen Gordon, Natasha Kimmet, and everyone at Shambhala Publications for their work in improving the manuscript and shepherding the project through the publication process—and for their patience in working with this new author. I also want to thank Jill Rogers for her skilled copyediting.

My parents, siblings, nieces, nephews, in-laws, and friends filled my life with love and provided welcome opportunities to deepen my understanding of the Buddha's teachings.

During the writing of this book, my longtime friend Tom Chung-Tong Lee passed away after battling cancer. His life touched mine in numerous ways even though we lived on different continents. The generosity of his spirit can be found in many pages of this book.

David Slaymaker, my husband who introduced me to Chan practice and taught me how to meditate years ago, championed me throughout the long process. He sustained me with his unconditional support and love. He helped me think through important decisions about writing and publishing and gave me space when I needed to hide away to write. His loving support makes my Dharma work, not just this book, possible. I could not ask for a better life partner.

My late teachers Chan Master Sheng Yen and Dr. John Crook, and my current teacher Dr. Simon Child, taught me Dharma, Chan practice, and how to be a teacher. Training and working with them have been among the greatest blessings of my life. Everything you find useful in this book came from their teachings and examples. This book is dedicated to them with my deepest gratitude.

NOTES

1. Chan Master Sheng Yen, *The Poetry of Enlightenment: Poems by Ancient Chan Masters* (Boston: Shambhala, 2006), 90.
2. Taigen Dan Leighton, *Cultivating the Empty Field: The Silent Illumination of Zen Master Hongzhi* (Rutland, VT: Tuttle Publishing, 2000), 31.
3. Sheng Yen, *The Poetry of Enlightenment*, 90.
4. Master Sheng-Yen with Dan Stevenson, *Hoofprint of the Ox: Principles of the Chan Buddhist Path as Taught by a Modern Chinese Master* (Oxford: Oxford University Press, 2001), 142.
5. Sheng Yen, *The Poetry of Enlightenment*, 90.
6. John Welwood, "Human Nature, Buddha Nature," interview by Tina Fossella, *Tricycle*, Spring 2011, https://tricycle.org/magazine/human-nature-buddha-nature/.
7. A. F. Price and Wong Mou-lam, trans., *The Diamond Sutra and The Sutra of Hui-Neng* (Boston: Shambhala, 1990), 39.
8. Chan Master Sheng Yen, *There Is No Suffering: A Commentary on the Heart Sutra* (Elmhurst, NY: Dharma Drum Publications and North Atlantic Books, 2001), 8.

9. Chan Master Sheng Yen, introduction to *Ming mo fo jiao yan jiu* (Research in Late Ming Buddhism) (Taipei: Dharma Drum Culture, 2000).

10. Chan Master Sheng Yen, *Attaining the Way: A Guide to the Practice of Chan Buddhism* (Boston: Shambhala, 2006), 152.

11. Andrew C. Hafenbrack, "An Unintended Consequence of Mindfulness," *Washington Post*, May 18, 2022, Outlook, https://www.washingtonpost.com/outlook/2022/05/18/mindful-meditation-guilt-amends/.

12. Dillard, Annie. *The Writing Life* (New York: HarperCollins, 2009), 32.

13. Sheng Yen, *The Poetry of Enlightenment*, 24.

14. J. C. Cleary, trans., *Swampland Flowers: The Letters and Lectures of Zen Master Ta Hui* (Boulder, CO: Shambhala, 2021), 89.

15. A. F. Price and Wong Mou-lam, *The Diamond Sutra and the Sutra of Hui-Neng*, 22–23.

16. Chan Master Sheng Yen, *Dharma Drum: The Life and Heart of Chan Practice* (Elmhurst, NY: Dharma Drum Publications, 1996), 187.

ABOUT THE AUTHOR

Rebecca Li, PhD, is the founder and guiding teacher of Chan Dharma Community. She began Buddhist practice in 1995 while in graduate school in California and took refuge with Chan Master Sheng Yen, founder of Dharma Drum Mountain, the same year. While in graduate school, she flew to New York to attend intensive retreats with Master Sheng Yen. She then moved to New Jersey to take an academic position and to be closer to her teacher, and in 1999 began serving as his translator and undergoing teacher training with him. She started teaching Dharma classes in 2002.

In 2001, Rebecca also began to study with Drs. John Crook and Simon Child, two of Master Sheng Yen's Dharma heirs. After Master Sheng Yen's passing in 2009 and John Crook's passing in 2011, she continued her work with Simon Child, who remains her current teacher. Over the years, Rebecca has co-led intensive Chan retreats with Simon Child and collaborated with other teachers in the Western Chan Fellowship of the United Kingdom.

In 2016, Rebecca received full Dharma transmission from Simon Child and became a third-generation Dharma heir in the Dharma Drum Lineage of Chan Master Sheng Yen, which combines the centuries-old Chan Buddhist lineages of Caodong and Linji (more commonly known by their Japanese equivalents, Soto and Rinzai). Her Dharma transmission name is Zhi-Deng Fa-Chuan (智燈法傳 Wisdom Lamp, Dharma Transmitting).

Currently, Rebecca offers meditation and Dharma classes, gives public lectures, and leads residential Chan retreats in North America and Europe. Her teachings have appeared in North American Buddhist publications including *Tricycle, Buddhadharma, Lion's Roar*, and *Chan Magazine,* as well as in Asian Buddhist publications such as *Humanity Magazine.* She is one of the founding board members of GenX Buddhist Teachers Sangha, whose mission is to foster cross-lineage support among Dharma teachers.

Rebecca is also a sociology professor and the author of *Allow Joy into Our Hearts: Chan Practice in Uncertain Times.* She lives with her husband in New Jersey. Her talks, writings, schedule, and guided meditations can be found at www.rebeccali.org.